L'Only Child
Dad's Side of the Story

L'Only Child
Dad's Side of the Story

Edward V. Mirabella

TATE PUBLISHING
AND ENTERPRISES, LLC

Published by Tate Publishing & Enterprises, LLC
127 E. Trade Center Terrace | Mustang, Oklahoma 73064 USA
1.888.361.9473 | www.tatepublishing.com

Tate Publishing is committed to excellence in the publishing industry. The company reflects the philosophy established by the founders, based on Psalm 68:11,
"The Lord gave the word and great was the company of those who published it."

Book design copyright © 2013 by Tate Publishing, LLC. All rights reserved.
Cover design by Rodrigo Adolfo
Interior design by Caypeeline Casas

Published in the United States of America

ISBN: 978-1-62994-096-0
Biography & Autobiography / Personal Memoirs
13.10.30

Dedication

For Dawn, Denise, Deana, Edward and Nicolle

Foreword

I started writing this book after I turned 58 and found myself looking back over my life. Maybe we all reach that point. I see things I would have done differently and wonder how those changes might have been reflected in the present day. I also realize that those thoughts, and any changes, are probably only dreams. I celebrated my 70th birthday a few months ago, and this writing is now complete. The pain of past memories stopped the process many times, but here it is, finally.

Yes, we can try to learn from the experiences of the past, but we seem to make the same mistakes all over again. I guess it's because of those earliest times of our lives, which pre-determine the path that each of us will take. This is the process that begins with birth, and those first few formative years that tend to imprint what the eventual path will be.

Did my parents love me? Definitely. Did they try to impress the basic values that were important to them on me? Of course they did. Was I taught that respect, responsibility and hard work are the pre-requisites for a fruitful life? The answer is again a resounding, "Yes."

They also taught me to pay for my mistakes in life, without hanging the blame on others. This is the one lesson I've learned all too well.

That's in stark contrast to the youth of today, who almost always find a reason to pass their mistakes on to some other person or set of circumstances. Society has become far more analytical, and attempts to dissect events in the ever-present need to understand them. In my youth there was no need to understand why I did what I did. Just the fact that I did something wrong was enough. You fucked up, Ed, was all I ever needed to understand. Don't do it again. No analysis was needed, because my parents and the establishment could never be wrong or even questioned. Why would they lead me down the wrong path? They only want the best for me. They only want to make me a better person. They only do things out of love for me. They only want me to benefit from the mistakes that they made. They only want me to be happy. I really believed all that, but somehow all of their best intentions didn't keep me from finding everything out for myself. And man, did I find out.

By the age of 17, I decided that I had enough of their teaching, and was determined to escape from their generation, their ideals and their unhappiness as I perceived it. I was about to embark on a crusade to be what I wanted to be. To do what I wanted to do, and answer to no one. I would create my own happiness, and accept full responsibility for my actions. Don't let anybody try to stop me either, because I know what I'm doing. Now, all these years later, I can truly state that my mistakes are my own.

Three marriages, two divorces and five children later, I see my children looking at me in much the same manner I did with my parents. How can that be? I grew up in the same home with both parents. My children didn't get that opportunity.

So many from my generation made it to the same place: Broken marriages, many followed by more of the same. Children that only saw Dad on the weekends, or an occasional vacation. Dad's new wife, or newest wife, with her kid or kids from her previous marriage or marriages in tow. Dad had so little time or money. Dad had more important things to do. Dad has a new wife and other kids now. Your Dad doesn't really care about us, or he would do more for us. I'm going to drag Dad's ass back into court again. Your Dad is going to pay for this and that and whatever else I can nail him for.

This evolution has taken the unhappy two-parent family to a new level, in which Dad is the only one wrong and to blame for everything that happens in life. He only cares about himself and his current circle of friends, family, or the slut he is sleeping with this week. Mommy's the only one that you can really count on, because she's the only one that really loves you.

So much has been written about single-parent families. I'd be hard pressed to find many situations where the head of the household is Dad. Much has been written about the effects of divorce on children. Most of that information was related by the custodial parent, who is almost always the mother. The court system almost always decides that what's best for the children is to be with the mother, and that Dad is best suited to fill the role of provider. In an age in which people scream about the unfairness of sexual discrimination in employment, the existence of a glass ceiling, equal pay for both sexes, there still seems to be an uneven playing field that sends dear old Dad into an arena where he will always be the proverbial underdog.

Out of this process we find a generation of children with all sorts of questions, conflicts and insecurities. They are torn between their parents like no generation before them. They have been used as pawns in a chess game that no one wins. The term "stalemate" takes on a whole new meaning. Each side is constantly trying to achieve the high ground with the kids. Mom has the advantage because she is with them most of the time. Dad has to undertake damage control during his visitation schedule, which is usually decided in a courtroom during the most-bitter part of the divorce process. The mom, as custodial parent, can for almost any reason alter that schedule. Let Dad try and he's met with a waving fist clenching a legal document.

Time usually diminishes the bitterness, and the name-calling fades in frequency, but the damage has been done. The children are in many cases scarred forever, and Dad gets tired of defending himself, because it sounds like a tennis ball going back and forth across the net. The volley can last for years.

The kids grow up and, with luck, move on with their lives and families. Dad is now a grandfather and, like any grandparent, provides advice from time to time. Sometimes the kids listen out of politeness or respect. Sometimes they remind you that they will decide what's best or right for their children. And sometimes you can detect a note of sarcasm or disbelief, "that Dad is actually trying to tell me how to raise my child. Just who the hell does he think he is, anyway?"

I think it's time for someone to tell Dad's side of the story.

CHAPTER

1

Feb. 23, 1983 and it's moving day. I stuff the last of my few possessions into the trunk and back seat of my car and take one last look at the place I've called home for the past seven years.

I remember buying the vacant lot in 1975 and the construction process that thrilled me to the bone every time I turned the corner and saw the changes that had taken place since my last visit the previous week. First the excavation, then the pouring of the foundation and the endless wait until the builder was sure the cement was ready to bear the weight of the frame and brick house it would support. Finally the framework was complete and the roof and shingles installed. The siding came next, and I was sure that the house would be finished in the next week or two. The interior work, with all the electric and plumbing, stretched my nerves to the limit as it looked as if the walls, plaster and paint would never get done. I tried to calm my impatience by taking pictures of each stage and laying them out on my kitchen table to track the progress and freeze the memories in an album forever. I wonder where those pictures are now? I guess they are still back in the house, there with so many other things I once thought were "mine or ours."

I'm not taking much with me on this move, because I'm the only one that's leaving. My two youngest children are staying with a friend so as not to witness the breakup of their Mom and Dad. My wife, Chris, is standing at the door doing her very best to alert the neighborhood of the abandonment she is being subjected to. I'm trying to make sense of the scene, because we had agreed that a separation was best just 24 hours ago. We had met with an attorney to try to ensure a smooth process, from separation through divorce. One lawyer is certainly cheaper than two, and I had agreed to all of her conditions anyway. I admitted that I wanted out, and would be willing to pay the price for my decision. We would put the children first, so as not to cause them any emotional stress, and try to maintain the status quo. They would continue to live in the same house with their mother, visitation would be liberal, and all disagreements would be settled when the children weren't around.

To keep those promises, I had rented a one-bedroom apartment in a complex not 10 minutes away. I had promised to stay in Nassau County to be close to the kids. I wouldn't need much more than a bed and some kitchen furniture. I'd sleep on the floor for a few nights until I could buy a bed. I'd eat out until I had time to make my own kitchen table, something I'd always wanted to do, anyway. I'd have plenty of time to do it, too, because I wouldn't have the resources to do much else. Yes, I would still have that chalet in the

Poconos, which we'd agreed I could keep in exchange for signing over my share of the house. Of course, I'd have to rent out the chalet to help meet my child support and alimony payments, but that wouldn't be for too long, right? I'm young enough to work hard, and I'm positive that my income level will continue to grow. In a few years I'll be back on my feet again.

My wife's voice is getting much louder now, and I have only one thing left to take from the house. At the attorney's office, I had asked for only one piece of furniture, a grandfather clock given to me by my mother. I had put my clothing in the car to cushion the clock. I maneuvered the clock through the front door and looked down the remaining steps. As I stepped down, I tripped over something and felt myself falling. I managed to maneuver so I would fall to the ground first with the clock on top of me, to cushion it from damage. I landed first with the clock on my chest and looked up to see a grin across my wife's face. She had tripped me.

Why was this happening? We had come to terms, had accepted the inevitable. This day was tough enough for all concerned, so I picked up my clock and myself and put both in the car. I had to get away from there now. I drove away without looking through the rearview mirror. I had to get away from her, and as quickly as possible. We both needed time to heal. We both needed time to adjust.

Only one of us, it turned out, needed time to get even.

During the brief drive to my apartment, I tried to calm myself. I was already missing the kids. Eddie was eight years old now, Nicole was only five. Surely they would adjust to the new living arrangements if Chris and I worked at making it work. I lit a cigarette and found some soft music on the radio. I found myself thinking about the night in 1970 when I first met Chris at a club back in Brooklyn.

Several months before meeting Chris, I had separated from my first wife. Again, I left two children behind. Dawn was only three years old and Denise had just been born. I left with the clothes on my back, a suitcase that contained whatever else I owned and $15 in my pocket. Instead of driving away in my car, I rode away on a bus. Instead of renting an apartment, I went back to my parents' house. It was my first wife's decision to separate and I swore I would never let it happen to me again. And yet here it was, happening again. It's like the same bad dream you suffer through night after night. Each time your mind races to find a way to change the ending, but you can't. Each time you try to awaken to stop the dream, because the end is too hard to bear.

I don't remember the drive, but I found myself pulling into the parking lot of the apartment complex. I parked outside the front door and looked up at the two windows that would be mine to look out of, suddenly starting to feel sorry for myself. C'mon Ed, it's time to unload. It looks like rain. It's also Dawn's 17th birthday.

An hour later, I'm standing in the middle of an empty room. My business suits are hung in the closet, and the shoes are neatly lined up on the closet floor. The rest of my belongings are in boxes or bags piled against one wall. Nowhere to put them right now! I walk into the kitchen and stare at the open, but empty, refrigerator. No matter, I'm not hungry anyway. I see the phone out of the corner of my eye and reach for it in the hope that it has been connected. The dial tone makes me smile, knowing I can call the little ones back in East Meadow, but first I have to call Dawn to wish her a happy birthday. I can't tell her what's happened right now, but I have to tell her something. I don't want her or Denise to try to reach me back at the house. I dial slowly and Dawn picks up the phone. Hi, honey, happy birthday. As usual, Dawn makes me feel like the most important person in the world. She possesses that special unconditional love that I often feel I don't deserve. I ask her how she spent the day and apologize for not seeing her today, because I'm out of town on business. I promise to come to Staten Island on the weekend to take her and Denise out to lunch. She forgives me immediately, and says that she understands. She always understands. It's her nature. In the back of my mind I'm thinking about her desire to go to college. One more year of high school! Not enough time for me to get back on my feet. I always intended to put money aside for her and her sister, but I got caught up in the thought that there was plenty of time to plan for college.

I was married to Chris less than two years after Betty and I separated, and put most of my energy into proving that I was a good husband and father. I never quite figured out just who I was proving it to. I know that I never really recovered from Betty's request for a divorce. Our courtship was filled with the kind of turmoil that should have provided a clue as to what kind of a marriage we would end up with. Betty has two sisters who had a scary kind of control over her. They never approved of me right from the start, and I can remember the several times Betty returned the engagement ring. Within several days and sometimes hours the ring was back on her hand, but the control that her sisters had over her never went away. She looked up to them. They were older, married and had kids of their own. They had cared for Betty after their mother died, when Betty was only 10. The sisters were several years older, and assumed the role of co-mothers. The attempt was noble, but both of them were scarred beyond repair from what they endured as kids.

Betty was too little to remember those times, her mother dying from cancer and the alcoholic father who found his courage, and fury, in a bottle of Scotch. When I met her, her father was re-married and Betty was living with her Dad and stepmother in what appeared to be a fairly happy and stable family environment. Several months later, at a family celebration, I began to realize the transformation that took place after her Dad had a few drinks. The combination of alcohol and diabetes, and the frustration and anger the alcohol released, turned him into something I wanted no part of. I had never witnessed anything like it growing up at home. Make no mistake—my mother and father fought plenty, but drinking was an infrequent event in our house, and my father never struck my mother or me, even though, on occasion, we gave him plenty of reason to. Thinking about those times, I wonder why I went through with a marriage that was destined to fail.

Her sisters never let up on her, and three years and two children later, Betty wanted out. Fourteen years later, the similarities between the first and second marriages are frightening.

I finished my conversation with Dawn, and after saying a quick hello to Denise, hung up the phone. I stared at it for awhile, trying to get up the courage to call Eddie and Nicole. I needed to hear their voices, but I knew I would have to get past Chris first. So be it. The phone rang, but there was no answer. Maybe it's for the best, I thought. I'll call tomorrow, when I get to the office. It was getting dark and I knew I should get something into my stomach. Did I eat anything today? I don't think so.

I discover the local deli is well stocked with the basics, although the prices are much higher than at the supermarket. I buy only what I need for the morning: juice, coffee, milk, bread, butter and eggs. I order a sandwich for my supper and a bottle of Coke. On the way back to the apartment, I stop at a local department store to buy a pillow. Make that two pillows, a blanket and an air mattress. I rationalize that I will need these things when the kids come for an overnight visit, and for the next several days, I'll use them. I'll get paid tomorrow, and I'll buy a bed right after work. Back at the apartment, I realize I don't have any light in the bedroom. The kitchen has a ceiling fixture, but the rest of the apartment is dark. I don't have an alarm clock or clock radio, either. I call my secretary at home and ask her to phone me in the morning, in the event I don't wake up on time. I finish the sandwich and plug in the small portable TV I had taken from the workshop in my garage. I set up my bed on the living room floor. I try to sleep, but the events of the past several days keep my mind busy. I remember looking at my watch at 2 a.m. Soon the phone rings and it's my secretary, Debbie. "It's time to get up, Ed."

Dad the newlywed 1940

CHAPTER

2

As I pulled into the parking lot at the office, I started to think that the next eight hours would allow me to focus on my job. That notion was quickly dismissed as I walked into the office. Debbie met me at the door, with a sympathetic look on her face. "Your attorney, Mr. McGowan, is holding and needs to speak to you immediately." This can't be good, I thought, as I shut the door to my office and picked up the phone. I listened to him as he explained that Chris had retained her own attorney the minute I closed the door behind me the previous day. She was now charging me with abandonment.

"Since I don't specialize in divorce, I suggest you retain another attorney as soon as possible," my attorney said. He closed the conversation with a "good luck," and I thought that's exactly what I was going to need. My verbal agreement with Chris was apparently null and void, and I was now facing the long, drawn-out divorce battle I had wanted to avoid. I'll search out a new attorney later in the day, I thought, but right now I need to call Mom and tell her what's going on. I would not focus much on work that day, and would find that work would take a backseat for years to come.

Calling Mom wasn't an easy process because she is totally deaf and a lip reader. She lost the last of her hearing at age 16 and had perfected lip reading quite by accident. Her hearing loss was gradual, so gradual that she wasn't fully aware of it until a high school teacher asked her to write something on the blackboard. As he instructed her, she kept looking over her shoulder and directly at him. He told her, "Don't look at me, look at the blackboard." It was at that instant that she realized that her hearing loss was almost total. That epiphany explained why her grades had plummeted during the past year, and the ensuing grief brought down on her by my grandfather. He demanded nothing but perfection from his children, although he never stopped to think that he was far from perfect in many ways.

To communicate with Mom by phone, I purchased a TTY, a Telephone Typewriter. I would dial her number and place the phone on the cradle. Her phone would ring, and activate blinking lights in her house, telling her that a call was coming in. She would pick up her phone and place it in the cradle of her TTY and type "Hello this is Mae. Who is calling?" The ensuing conversation would be lengthened by the time it took for me to type my message, and more time for her to type a reply. The lettering would dart across the viewing screen, and ultimately she could have a phone conversation. It was remarkable technology for 1983.

Needless to say, I should have gone to see her face to face. This wasn't going to be a pleasant call. The news I needed to deliver was bad, but of course she would say that she had been right all along, and I should have listened to her, and on and on. Mom didn't approve of wife No. 1 or wife No. 2, and quite frankly, didn't approve of many things during the course of my life. The ensuing conversation was as I expected, but at least now she knew, and in a matter of minutes her entire world would know about my latest failure, because her sisters and friends had their own TTYs so they could communicate with Mae by phone. What a glorious time this would be for her. She could tear Chris apart without any fear of reprisal, and remind all that would listen—well, read—that her son Edward had made another huge mistake.

Why did he marry a second time, and have more children? Answer: He was running away from you, Mom.

CHAPTER

3

Mom's handicap meant she received special treatment from family and friends. Her ability to lip read was regarded as something of a miracle. She was never taught the process, but simply assimilated it over several years. As her hearing deteriorated, her eyes started to focus on a person's mouth. Back in the 1930s, she had contracted diphtheria, and one of the remnants of the illness was what's called "nerve deafness." Once the problem was diagnosed, her father took her to every specialist he could find in an attempt to reverse the process and ultimately restore her hearing. That was not to be, and her father ultimately had to settle for the fact that he had created a child with the rare ability to overcome a severe handicap. Her speech was normal, and as long as you looked directly at her and spoke in a normal, unrushed fashion, she could read your lips and carry on a normal conversation.

There were ancillary benefits to being a lip reader, as well: Mom could spy on conversations that she wasn't a part of. Very often in restaurants or the supermarket she would focus on other people, and later recount the conversation she had "overheard." I have vivid memories of one such conversation when I was riding into Manhattan for a job interview at Bankers Trust Company. I was 20 years old and had just received a hardship separation from the Navy, after my Dad became paralyzed. I was headed to 16 Wall Street, and Mom worked for a title company just around the corner. We rode into the city together, and I noticed Mom was muttering something about that "son of a bitch." Her eyes were fixed on a grey-haired business-man seated next to a very attractive young woman who appeared to be 30 years his junior. Mom took in the entire conversation during the course of the train ride, and when the train pulled into Wall Street, she got up and walked directly over to the young woman, and told her she could do much better with a man her own age. I'll never forget the looks on their faces—or the smile on Mom's.

The ability to lip read also had a down side. Many times she would pick up parts of other peoples conver-sations that she wasn't supposed to. Very quickly, family members and friends learned to make sure their back was facing Mom when they were involved in a conver-sation that wasn't meant for her "ears."

Early on, she learned that her handicap could be a very useful tool in all her relationships. Her favorite phrase became, "You have to understand that I am deaf." What does a two-year-old boy know about under-standing the needs and problems associated with her affliction? Apparently I didn't have a choice in the mat-ter, and I didn't have a normal childhood or upbringing as a result. From the age of two, I was expected to be her eyes and ears when her back was turned. If she had difficulty reading lips because the person mumbled or had a mustache, I had to listen to the conversation and then repeat it to her. I had to stay in the house with her when Dad was out, because the phone might ring and I would have to answer it for her and relay the conversation to her. I never doubted that she loved me, but I became her personal crutch, and as the years went by it became increasingly stressful. It was always about her needs, and not about a little boy who just wanted to be a child in the normal sense.

Growing up in Brooklyn, I never had many close friends, because Mom looked at all of them as a threat. No one could take me away from her for very long, or she found reasons to decide that I shouldn't be allowed to associate with them. If some ignorant person, young or old, made the mistake of smiling at her handicap, that person was no longer allowed to be my friend or hers. She wanted to choose my friends when I was young, and wanted to choose my wife later on. It was ultimately the rebellion in me that led to my mistakes.

As an only child I envied my cousins and friends that had a sister or a brother. Was Mom selfish in only producing one child? A second one could have shared the burden, and maybe each of us could have enjoyed at least half of our formative years, but that was not to be. I also was intimately aware of the horrors of child birth, and the damage it caused to parts of the body that I still can't think about or visualize until this day. I found myself thinking at an early age that I had brought much pain to my mother, and later on in life it was no different. I was still making her unhappy.

When I think about my Dad, I feel great love and, at times, greater contempt. He suffered much as I did dealing with a wife that constantly used her handicap to keep him in line. My memories reveal a man who was soft and pleasant, worked hard and loved three things: his son, good food and, most of all, his wife Mae. His greatest goal and challenge was to make her happy, which he never achieved. You see, Mom married beneath her station. She was second-generation American on her mother's side, and her father, John, was a practicing attorney. He never bothered to take the bar exam, actually, but that's another story. You could get away with things like that in the 1920s and '30s.

Dad emigrated from Italy in 1912 at the age of four, with his mother Catarina and four half-sisters. His father, Carmelo, had married Catarina and taken on the responsibility of her four children from a prior marriage. My father was the only child they had together, and was looked upon by his siblings as their step dad's son, not as their brother. Because he was so much younger than his siblings, he found himself solely responsible for his mother's well being at the age of 16, when his father died. Dad left school having only completed the eighth grade. As a child I can only remember a hand- ful of times I visited with his siblings. Mom controlled that aspect of our lives also. She was happy when he did what she wanted, and the few times Dad prevailed, she let him know in no uncertain terms that his life would be miserable as a result.

An example from when I was 10 or 11: I had a part time job working at a local Laundromat. I didn't get paid to deliver laundry to the customers, but relied on tips. I was always a skinny little kid and wore eyeglasses, and I guess the sight of me lugging a laundry bag up five flights of stairs in the local apartment houses worked to my advantage. Tips ranged from nothing or a nickel to a quarter, and I found that I could earn as much as a dollar a day. I saved that money, and even opened a savings account at the local bank. My dream was a knife for my tackle box that I could use to cut bait or fishing line. Dad often worked six days a week, but on the rare occasion he had a Saturday off, he would take me to Coney Island, where we fished off Steeplechase Pier. We never caught anything worth noting, or eating for that matter, but our outings were always very special times for me.

Several days before one fishing trip, Dad told Mom he was taking me to Woolworth's to buy a small knife for the tackle box, with money I had saved. She forbade him to do it. He stood up to her and we bought the knife. She tortured him for days after, and then everything seemed to subside. Several weeks later, Dad and I were preparing for our day of fishing. On a Friday evening after supper we were out in the yard seated at a wooden table sorting hooks and sinkers for the next day. I took the knife out of the tackle box to cut some line and placed it down on the table. Mom suddenly appeared over my left shoulder and picked up the knife to look at it. She asked if this was the knife that I had bought despite her protests. I nodded yes, and watched her plunge the knife into the wooden table top in front of me, then bend it quickly, snapping the blade. She looked at Dad and said, "Now I'm happy," and walked into the house. Dad never said a word, I felt my eyes fill with tears, and I can remember thinking just how much I hated her at that moment. That event has lived with me all these years. Unfortunately, there were many more events leading up to the knife incident and many more to come.

When I turned five, my mother decided that it was time for me to go to school. I thought kindergarten would be fun, and I would attend with other neighborhood kids I knew. In September 1948, I walked into school with my mom. She stopped just inside the doors and told me that I should tell anyone who asked that I was six, not five. She went on to explain that kindergarten was a waste of time. "You learn nothing but finger-painting and spend most of your time playing with blocks," she said. She then told me that I was starting first grade that day, although I was a full year and a half younger than my new classmates. I was also a scrawny little guy who was always in the front of the line, because I was not only the youngest, but also the shortest. I remember wanting to tell the teacher my real age, but knew what I would face if I did. I was always lectured about the virtues of telling the truth, and here I was expected to lie because Mom thought it was the right thing to do. How will I know when it's OK to lie in the future? I guess it will be OK if it helps to achieve a specific goal.

My first day of school was indeed a preview of what was to come. I immediately made mistakes that resulted in several reprimands from the teacher. I couldn't get used to raising my hand to be recognized because I'd spent the first five years of my life adjusting to mom's handicap. For example, I would leave my seat and walk to the front of the classroom and tap the teacher on the arm, as I always did with my Mom. I also spoke slowly and clear, moving my mouth as I did at home, where Mom needed to read my lips. I was quickly categorized as a child with behavioral problems. My teacher had no idea my Mom was deaf and a lip-reader. Several days later, Mom was summoned to school and explained why I did things "differently." When I got home that day feeling better about things, Mom told me that I was to be punished for embarrassing her, and then added the words that always put fear in me: "On Sunday we are going to visit your Grandfather. He will know what to do with you."

She would never admit that bypassing kindergarten was a mistake.

Grandpa Natoli and his wife Nani—hers was bastardized Italian for what should have been pronounced "Nonna"—lived on the third floor of the house they owned in South Brooklyn. The lower floors were rented out to help make ends meet. The building was in bad shape and needed all sorts of repairs, none of which, when made, ever made the place look any better. If you were family, you only went there for special occasions like a birthday or a death in the family. Nani was a second-generation American, one of five children raised in New Jersey, though poorly educated. Grandpa was a well-spoken, self-educated immigrant with no discernible Italian accent, which amazes me to this day. He tried his hand at many things, but became "Mister John" in the Italian community in which he lived. He was wise and shrewd, and assisted the immigrants with citizenship issues, negotiated dowry payments, and at one time in the 1920s, was an advisor to a well known mob boss. He could bullshit anyone and get away with it. He knew his way around the courthouse in Brooklyn so well that even judges believed his claim that he was an attorney.

Payment for his services was rarely in cash. Much more likely was a barrel of homemade wine, a crate of chickens or other livestock, including baby lambs and goats, which were tied to the fence in the yard until Mr. John pointed to the animal and proclaimed, "Sunday dinner." My mother and her two sisters and brother treated the lambs and goats as pets, only to be served Billy the Goat the next Sunday. As children they were traumatized by these events, but Grandpa wouldn't stand for it. "You sit at the table and eat, or you go to bed without dinner, and of course, a beating to boot." His word was the law, including rules for everyone that he alone could violate if it served his purpose. I guess the term "tyrant" fits him best. His wife and children respected him out of fear, until poor health made him homebound during the last 15 years of his life. Nani had left him several times because of his violent temper or his attraction to younger women. She always came back, and the last time she moved back to the old house, it was to care for him in his final years.

I remember walking into the living room that Sunday, and looking at Grandpa, seated in his usual chair by the window. He still wore the white shirt with the removable collar. The shirt was worn for many days back then, but the starched cardboard collar was put on when he went out on business. His suspenders were dark blue and his slacks a dark grey wool that must have itched something terrible. He was thin and wiry, and possessed the darkest deep-set eyes I have ever seen. His eyes were shielded by bushy black eyebrows and he always seemed to have a two-day beard. The room was furnished with belongings from a better time, and the smell of cigar smoke was omnipresent. He seldom left his chair then, usually only to eat his meals in the kitchen, where he would use a linen napkin while the rest of us settled for paper. He'd then return to his seat by the window. I guess he would watch the world go by, and wonder where he had made a wrong turn during his life.

I hugged him and kissed him on the cheek, which was expected, and then sat across from him while Mom related the events of the prior week at school. My father stood in the background and never said a word. He just looked down at the floor. I wondered why my father was letting this happen. None of my cousins were ever brought in front of Grandpa for his "Italian medicine." He looked at me for what seemed like forever, looked out the window, puffed on the cigar, exhaled slowly, looked at the cigar in his hand, and then he started to speak. Until this day I can't remember a single word, only the intensity of those dark sunken eyes, and those demonic eyebrows. He never struck me, and at the end of each Sunday Session, and there were many of them from first grade through high school, he would say, "Now be a good boy, and don't let me hear about this again. This time you got off easy."

As I got older, I would challenge my mother when she used the "Grandpa threat," but not when I was five. I was glad it was over and we were going home. It wasn't over by a long shot, of course, as my folks got into a major argument over the day's events that culminated in one of my mother's many fainting spells, which always won the battle for her. I knew she would bolster the story and tell it over and over to anyone who would listen, and I would face repeat performances in front of my aunts, my uncle and, worst of all, my older cousins, all of whom thought they had the right to discipline the family problem child.

Fainting, by the way, was mere warm-up for Mom. In crescendo, she would lock herself in the bathroom and threaten to overdose on whatever was in the medicine cabinet until Dad removed the hinges from the door to rescue her. Quite a show for a five-year-old.

As I grew older, I started to resent my father for being weak. In reality, he was a sweet man who always worked hard and kept his mouth shut. He would stammer badly when he was upset, which brought jokes and ridicule from my mother and others in the family. In

1966, at the age of 58, he finally got even with Mom. But more about that later on.

Mom and Nani 1943

CHAPTER

4

I graduated from high school in June 1960, three months after my 17th birthday. I really had no peer group, as my classmates were all 18 or 19 years of age. They were driving and going to clubs on the weekends, while I was looking for an escape from that house at 424 East 7th Street in Flatbush. I wanted to attend college, but Mom said I wasn't college material, judging by my grades. True, I was not a good student. My head was always somewhere else—mostly thinking about the day I would be old enough to make my own decisions. I looked at each passing day as one day closer to achieving my dream.

Finally graduation day came, and I asked if I could go out later that night with a few friends who were a year behind me in school. It was usually the bowling alley on Church Avenue. In those days, you had to be 16 to bowl at night. I had been 16 until a short three months before, and the few friends I had were reveling in their ability to bowl at night. The rest of the graduating class was out at the local bars. I could only look in the window and wish I was there. They were driving, while I took the bus. Again, I should have gone to kindergarten. Mom was adamant. "You want to be with your friends instead of your mother and father," she said. Dad tried to intervene with a "let him go," but Mom silenced him with a quick "Shut up, Ang." He didn't say another word, but gave me the "I tried look."

I worked a full time job the rest of the summer and, despite my mother's misgivings, started classes at the local community college that fall. In December of that year I was called to the dean's office and advised that my grandfather had died. In January, I found a full-time job, then enlisted in the Naval Reserve right after my 18th birthday. This time Dad stood by my side and defended my right to make my own decisions. "You see, Mae, we can't stop him now that he's 18, and he will be home for another six months before he goes on active duty," he said. I was getting so close to my dream.

It was actually another year before I went on active duty. Mom didn't make the time pass easily, but I countered some of the trouble by threatening to make the military a career. After basic training, I was assigned to the USS Enterprise, the first nuclear-powered aircraft carrier. I remember boarding the ship for the first time, duffle bag over my shoulder, requesting permission to board, and then finding my way to my berth several decks below the hangar bay. I had some clerical skills and was assigned to what the Navy calls Ship Stores. In the Army, it's called Supply. I had a desk, a phone and a typewriter. Three days later, we were headed to the Mediterranean, with stops in Italy and France to come. It was a great time to be in the military, with no wars to worry about, and abundant time to go ashore and see the sights. Most of the sights were inside the bars, and many of us never managed to travel more than a half-mile from the dock.

We were usually transported to shore in liberty launches, which were small boats that could seat about 30 sailors. In bad weather we would board helicopters for the five-minute ride to shore. The Enterprise—better known as the "Big E"—was too large to tie up at the pier, hence the need for a shuttle of some sort. Once ashore, we wandered around aimlessly until one of the locals would offer to be our "guide," for a price of course. Military pay went a long way in the Mediterranean countries in those days. Food and drink cost what amounted to pennies. The big expense was incurred buying the local ladies a glass of colored water they called Champagne. They would sit with you, flatter you, and ultimately entice a sailor to venture upstairs for some one-on-one time. I was 19 at the time, skinny as a rail, and I obviously looked vulnerable to the waterfront scam artists. To my benefit, however, I didn't trust people easily; it had to be earned. I learned that lesson back home, from none other than my mother. I ultimately survived my first "Med Cruise," with good memories of some bad hangovers, and a wish to return again, so I could do it right next time.

Several months later, back in Norfolk, I was granted liberty and came home to Brooklyn for a couple weeks of leave. I was looking forward to hanging out with my friends in my dress uniform, and the opportunity to enjoy the positive attention members of the military were afforded in those days. Though World War

II had ended in 1945, the memory of the sacrifices made by our service members was still very much in the minds, and hearts, of the American people. That would change later, as the Vietnam War played out, as the peace movement gained steam and the news of Mai Lai and other atrocities leaked out, but the early 1960s were still a grand time to be in uniform.

I was home for 10 days when the so-called Cuban Missile Crisis broke out, and vacationing military personnel within 400 miles of their home base were called back to duty. That's another great thing about Brooklyn: It happens to be 450 miles from Norfolk, and I was allowed to complete my leave. When I returned to base, however, I was swiftly loaded onto a small plane normally used to carry the mail, and several hours later found myself in Guantanamo Bay, still attired in my dress—blue "woolen" uniform despite 90-plus degree temperatures. A group of us were kept on base for three days before finally boarding a destroyer that rendezvoused with the Enterprise somewhere in the Caribbean.

Working in Ship Stores very often resulted in the need to transfer supplies from one ship to another while at sea. This exercise required the two captains to maintain identical speed and cruise side by side while the supplies were "high lined" from one vessel to the other using a system of ropes and pulleys. These ropes and pulleys were manned by dozens of sailors that had to keep both ropes and cargo above the water level until the supplies were safely aboard the adjoining vessel. In this case, yours truly and two dozen other sailors were the cargo, and the ship-to-ship transfer I had taken part in so many times before became deadly serious. I fought to control my emotions—not to mention my bowels and bladder—while I was strapped into a chair that was hanging from the rope, that was attached to the pulleys, that was spread out between the two ships, that had to maintain identical speed and distance while dozens of hung-over sailors promised to keep my ass from the bottom of the ocean. Of course, that wasn't nearly interesting enough for the assembled crew, which decided to send two sailors across the open expanse of angry sea at the same time, thus completing the task in half the time. My "suicide buddy" was a black man with deep Baptist roots. His only words during our ride across the expanse were "Oh, Lordy," which he screamed repeatedly for the entire ride. My fear turned to laughter, then terror as my feet briefly brushed the top of the waves. By the end of the transfer I had turned religious myself, yelling "Thank you, Jesus!" while hugging my Baptist co-transportee.

We spent 56 days at sea as the crisis escalated into the U.S. naval blockade of Cuba, bringing America and the Soviet Union to the brink of nuclear Armageddon before the Russians finally blinked.

Meanwhile, back at home, Mom and Dad were entertaining a sailor from another ship that had come home with me on a weekend pass several months before. Bill was left parentless as a baby, grew up in an orphanage and joined the Navy when he turned 18. In my mother's eyes, he appreciated her more than I did, a sentiment she expressed in a letter to me while I was still at sea. Another arrow in my heart.

I fell ill the next time I came home on leave, and after several days was diagnosed with hepatitis by the family doctor—who still made house calls. The Navy sent an ambulance to pick me up, and I was transported to St. Albans Naval Hospital, where I spent the next 90 days recovering. What a wonderful time that was: Mom could visit me every other day. By comparison, my high line experience wasn't so bad after all.

5

After three months, it was time to return to active duty, knowing the length of my recuperation meant I would be reassigned to another ship. I reported back to Norfolk feeling very uneasy about my Dad. He wasn't feeling well the past few months, suffering from bad headaches. I remember his visits to St. Albans, when he spent hours in a reclining chair trying to ease the pounding pain. Several weeks after I returned to duty he was hospitalized with bleeding ulcers caused by the pain killer he was taking for the headaches. He recuperated from ulcer surgery very quickly, but was still plagued by the headaches.

My new ship, the USS Forrestal, would be leaving for the Mediterranean in 24 hours. I would have a second chance to see more of Italy, France and Spain. I promised myself that I would visit the cultural sites this time, and stay clear of the waterfront dives that attract most sailors.

The night before the ship was to leave, I received a call from the commanding officer with news passed on from my uncle Tom, brother to my mother. Dad had suffered a stroke, caused by a brain aneurysm, and was in serious condition. My uncle was advised to contact the American Red Cross, who would plead my case for emergency leave. I could not be released from the ship until that step was initiated through Naval Operations. The next morning the ship, with me on it, pulled away from the dock in Norfolk and headed for open sea. Several hours later I was advised to pack a bag and get up to the flight deck, where a Navy chopper was waiting to fly me back to Norfolk. I looked out the window and watched the ship get smaller and smaller. I knew at that moment that I'd never see the Mediterranean again, and my days in the Navy were about to come to an end. I had spent 11 months on active duty, and was granted a Hardship Separation several weeks later. Mom had pleaded her case to the Red Cross in a very convincing manner. Her handicap combined with me being the only child sealed the deal. Dad could never work again, but could lead a fairly normal life after a surgical procedure stopped the leaking artery. I was now the man of the family and had to be Mom's ears for an indefinite period of time. I'd been hearing those words since I was two years old, but now at age 20 they became more ominous. Her handicap hadn't stopped her from working in a Manhattan title company while I was in high school. The only thing she couldn't do was answer the phone. Her concentration level was high because she wasn't distracted by noise or the people around her, which resulted in high productivity.

Back in those days I was saddled with the responsibility of dusting and vacuuming the house after school, on alternate days. When she came home from work, she would run her white gloves over the surface of the furniture to determine if I'd completed my chores, which included setting the table and whatever else she could think of to keep me in the house. Most days she found some dust, which resulted in my being grounded for days. Another way of exercising total control over me. Each night at dinner, Dad and I had to listen attentively while she recounted the day's events, and how well liked and respected she was at work. Dad would only look down when she mentioned the names of the male coworkers that seemed to flirt with her on a daily basis. Those men were educated and truly appreciated her. I felt my father's pain every time she would remind him of the fact that she had married beneath her station in life. That was the way she controlled him. His love for her was unconditional and she knew it. She especially enjoyed talking about her one "true love," who had been forced to break it off with her by his parents because of her handicap.

I sat at the table taking all of this in. I know it hurt my Dad deeply, and I began to believe that I must be flawed as a result of their union. Dad was uneducated and downright stupid in her eyes, and she was a self centered ruthless person who had special rights and privileges because of her handicap. What could I expect from me?

After dinner I was expected to dry the dishes and put them away. God help me if I didn't dry them correctly. "If I was blessed with a daughter instead of a son, she would help with these chores," my mother liked to bemoan. I caught a slap in the face when, out of frustration, I suggested that she get pregnant again and hope for a girl. Dad giggled at my comment and caught a dirty look from Mom. I was again reminded that childbirth—my birth, in fact—was the most horrible experience she could recall. She was the recipient of 78 stitches and couldn't walk for weeks. I was only six pounds at birth. Was I born wearing a football helmet? Through the years the story of my birth became more graphic, and at last count she had received 176 stitches to close the wound caused by my entry into the world.

With Dad, 1944

CHAPTER

6

Now at 20 I was back in the nest. I got home on a Friday in May of 1963. My aunts, uncles and cousins were at the house with Mom, there to remind me that "Your mother needs you now more than ever." Mom smiled while they told me what was expected. On Monday, I was to get a learner's permit to drive, since "You see, you will have to take her everywhere now," they said. On Tuesday, Mom had arranged an interview for a job at a bank. A bank? I didn't want to work at a bank. I wanted to go back to college or maybe take the test for the Police Department. But the die was cast, there was to be no discussion. I would attend the interview, and God help me if I didn't get that job.

That first weekend home was normal. When I mentioned going out to see friends, the rant was instant: "You want to go out with your friends while your father is in the hospital?" "I need you to make phone calls for me." "I can't believe you would leave me at home alone." "What if your father takes a turn for the worst?" Unfairly as it sounds, I found myself resenting my Dad. Because of him, I was now trapped. I was going to be there all day, every day. And now the nights belonged to her, too.

I watched TV that Friday night at home, and caught the 11 p.m. news. There was a television crew outside the gates of Sing Sing Prison, waiting for the release of the nationally known bank robber, Willie Sutton. A young reporter by the name of Gabe Pressman pushed a microphone in front of Sutton and asked, "Why did you rob banks, Willie?" He replied, "That's where the money, is kid."

That's where the money is. I decided I'd go on for that job interview after all.

I reported to Bankers Trust Company at 16 Wall Street in Manhattan the following Monday morning, and was interviewed by Bob Potterfield in what was then called Personnel. The interview was relaxed in nature, with much discussion about my time in the Navy, and the concerned questions about my father's recovery. Mom worked with Mr. Potterfield's sister, so he was well aware of mom's handicap and her lip reading expertise. "You must be very proud of your mother," he said. "Her lip reading is truly a marvel."

Yes, and she was also well regarded by her supervisor, who thought her work ethic was superb. I knew all that because I was told about it on a daily basis. I never got the chance to brag about Mom, because she felt the need to do that herself. No one ever seemed to focus on the intense pressure that was placed on me from the time I was two years old. Silver lining: I didn't recognize at that point that I was honing communication skills that would serve me well during the next four decades I spent in the banking industry.

I was hired the same day, but continued to attend interviews and training classes until I was ultimately assigned to a branch office located in Brooklyn, a bus ride from my home. Mom was hoping I would be working near her in Manhattan. Then, we could travel to and from work together every day and meet for lunch. God must have been listening to my prayers that day instead.

I slowly started to adjust to a normal work week, and my Dad had recovered enough to resume driving Mom around during the day. I started night classes at Brooklyn College and tried to develop a social life on the weekends. While I had been in the Navy a girl named Betty I knew from South Brooklyn started to correspond with me. I had a part time job at a supermarket in her neighborhood while I was in high school, and began to notice her frequent trips to the store each day, with all of them ending at my cash register. I was ultimately invited to a party and got to know her crowd. Active duty put the friendship on hold, but now that I was back in Brooklyn I reached out to her, and we started to date.

The relationship got serious very quickly, despite interference from both of our families. We didn't see it at the time, but our relationship was destined to fail. I had fallen in love with her and we were engaged several months later. I found that I had more freedom than ever and couldn't wait to get married and flee the nest at 424 East 7th Street once and for all. Betty lived with her Dad and stepmom, and from my perspective, we had much in common, mostly that we both wanted out of difficult family situations. We were married in May 1965, and after a Pocono Mountain honeymoon—nobody went to Aruba back then—we moved into a one-bedroom apartment on East 52nd Street in Brooklyn. We were a full half-hour's drive from our parents' homes, but it would prove to be much too close.

7

Nine months and 15 days after we were married, Dawn was born. I couldn't believe the thick, straight black hair that she was born with. She came home several days later, and we planned for the christening. With all the focus on the new addition to our family, things started to look good, but not for long.

Dawn was only six weeks old when the phone rang one night. Dad had suffered another stroke, and this time it was massive. He was rushed to Kings County Hospital and admitted to intensive care. A short time after his ulcer surgery, he had suffered a mild stroke and the doctors had discovered an aneurysm in his brain. To stop the flow of blood to the ballooning blood vessel, they placed a metal clip on the carotid artery, and sent him home. We had all known it was only a matter of time before the aneurysm ruptured, and that time had run out on the eve of Dawn's christening.

Dawn's christening went on as planned, with my oldest cousin, John, as godfather. My Dad had been my first choice. I felt it would give him something to feel good about, what with so many health issues to deal with. Dad convinced me that he was too old and sick and I'd be better off if I selected someone else. Looking back, it was a good decision, because John took the role seriously, and has maintained close ties with Dawn through her whole life.

Two days after the christening, Dad underwent brain surgery in an attempt to stop the bleeding. I remember asking the doctor what the prognosis was. My uncle Tom, my mothers' brother, was at my side. The doctor's reply left little to consider. "He's got three weeks without the surgery, but 10 to 15 years with the surgery," the doctor told us. I looked at my uncle, who had the same piercing eyes of my grandfather, and he nodded his agreement that dad should have the surgery.

The one question we didn't ask was relative to "quality of life" afterwards. That phrase didn't exist in 1966. Dad came through the surgery but was left paralyzed on his left side. His mental capacity was also seriously impaired. His emotions were out of control. Many times a laugh would turn to tears, and body tremors would erupt without notice. Many years later my uncle and I questioned our decision to put him through the surgery. Dad's life was a living hell for the next 11 years, and so was mine. I am not discounting what my mother went through during the first eight years when we kept him at home. That was her obligation to her husband, "for better or worse," but she never let up on me. The fact that I had a wife, a child, and a growing bank career didn't seem to matter. She needed my support regardless of my responsibilities. I once again silently cursed my parents for only having had one child. My childhood was a blur of unhappy memories, and now my adult life was in turmoil also. I questioned where my loyalty should go on a daily basis. I knew where it should go, but my mother didn't see it that way. The phone rang at all times of the day and night with real and perceived emergencies.

I dealt with the situation as best I could, as did Betty. We both remembered the jubilation when Dawn was born, and in 1968 we wanted to feel that euphoria again. After several months of trying, Denise was conceived and was born premature in August 1969. Betty came home but the baby stayed in the hospital for what seemed like an eternity. I worked the two jobs, dealt with Mom's constant demands and tried to be a father and a husband. There just wasn't enough time, energy or desire to keep it all together. Let's not forget about the interference from Betty's' sisters. I guess we both sort of surrendered to the situation, and I wasn't surprised when Betty asked for a divorce within weeks of Denise's birth.

Grandpa and Nani Natoli, 1944

CHAPTER

8

It was a dreary night when I found myself standing on Utica Avenue waiting for the bus. I had one suitcase and several suits on a hanger. I had $15 in my pocket, and only one place to go, although the price would be heavy. I was numbed by the chain of events, and of course felt like a total failure. Mom and Dad had sold the old house and moved into an apartment, a ground-floor unit that better accommodated the wheelchair to which Dad had been sentenced. During the previous three years I had perfected the art of moving Dad and his wheelchair up and down the stairs, leveraging my 135 pounds as a counter weight to Dad's 180 pounds, plus the weight of the wheelchair. I learned early on not to let anyone else try to navigate flights of steps with Dad and the wheelchair. The very first time I allowed it, he was dropped down eight steps, resulting in a very unnecessary trip to the hospital for stitches to close a head wound.

Trips to relatives' homes were rare, and on occasion when we went to a restaurant to celebrate some special occasion, we were looked upon as an annoyance, and on several occasions I overheard comments that resulted in at least two fights with people who thought it was their right to advise us that Dad should not be taken into a public place. On one occasion, I put Dad and Mom in the car, loaded the wheelchair into the trunk and went back into the restaurant to vent my anger. The owner saw me moving toward the man I had exchanged unpleasantries with and blocked my path. I don't think I could have won the fight, but at that point I didn't care.

In the new apartment Dad could navigate the wheelchair from room to room fairly easily. We didn't have to worry about him venturing too close to the stairway, and he could actually wheel himself outside to sneak an occasional cigarette, the likely source of his vascular disease in the first place.

On the day Betty and I separated, I had called my parents from a pay phone to tell them I needed a place to stay for awhile. I arrived an hour later and found my mother in true form. She never once considered what I was feeling at that point in time. She had known all along that this marriage would never work, but as usual I didn't listen to her. Now she had to deal with the embarrassment caused by her only child. How would she explain it to family and friends? She had forgotten that her younger sister had been through two divorces in a time when nobody got a divorce. You just stayed the course, no matter how bad the relationship had deteriorated. I thought to myself. "You mean like you and Dad"? Then she laid down the rules that I had to live by to stay in her home. At 25 years of age I had a curfew, restricted use of the phone, and of course I would have to pick up all those responsibilities that my father could no longer handle. After one week I was rescued by that aunt who had gone through divorce and stayed with her on Staten Island until I found a place of my own.

I was devastated by the breakup of my marriage, and went into a deep depression almost immediately. I sought help from a therapist, which only infuriated my mother all the more. Now her son was crazy on top of everything else. This chain of events became her problem, not mine. It was, as usual, all about her. I was expected to be perfect and had always disappointed her. Was it because of her handicap that she became obsessed with my missteps? Was I expected to be perfect because she wasn't? I didn't know the answers to those questions, but I did know that I needed to stay as far away from her as possible for as long as it took me to get my life back on track.

Those first few weeks with my aunt Sylvia were a good form of therapy. She acted as a buffer between me and my mother, and I tried to concentrate on my job at the bank and finding my own apartment. Within months, Betty and I signed the divorce decree and sold the house on East 52nd Street. She stayed in the Flatlands section of Brooklyn and I found an apartment several miles away. I was able to get a car loan, and took on a second job to make the monthly payments, and pay the rent. I was alone for the first time in my life and didn't appreciate it at all. I wasn't used to peace and quiet. I didn't know how to enjoy it.

On the weekends I tried to see my girls whenever possible, but the burden of the second job combined with my mother's ever-present demands left little time for the kids that so desperately needed both a mom and a dad. I was living up to my legal and financial obligations, but was frustrated by my inability to be the father I so badly wanted to be. They were too little to understand then, and I figured things would get easier over time and I would make it up to them. Things never got easier, and you can never make up for lost time. I still live with that.

CHAPTER

9

The toughest part of living alone back then involved the kids. I loved putting Dawn down for the night after her bath, enjoying the sweet smell of baby shampoo and those special hugs that only a father can appreciate. Little Denise would only share those times on overnight visits, which were few and far between. The friends Betty and I had had during our marriage weren't really friends anymore. They were all married couples, and didn't want the recently divorced guy or gal around. It seemed to make people uncomfortable. It also forced them to make a choice between us, and so they ultimately just stopped associating with us both.

The next year or two are a blurred vision of working, working some more, brief visitation, and many nights spent at the bars and clubs that permeated the Bay Ridge section of Brooklyn.

The Revelation Club was located directly across the street from the bank branch that I worked at in 1969. The owner of the club had approached me for financing. I was able to put a loan package together, and so was treated like a dignitary when the club opened. It started out as a supper club with entertainment, but quickly morphed into a stand-out night spot in an area of Brooklyn that had bars and restaurants on every corner.

The owner made sure I was introduced to all the employees and entertainers, and I received the very best of service along with the occasional free drink. The weekend crowd knew that I was somebody who "knew somebody," and friendships developed in a short amount of time. Maybe Mom was right when she urged me—no, pushed me—into banking. In those years, the community banker was the key to a business owner's financial needs, and I often had to decline the free lunch and other gratuities that were offered. I learned that nothing is for nothing, and my inherent lack of trust in people would be my best friend. I learned to trust my gut, and if my gut said, "something is wrong," my gut was right.

I was still a rookie in commercial banking, but the word got out pretty quickly about a young kid who was able to get the lending officers to sign off on his deals. I didn't let this newfound reputation go to my head, as I had seen a number of careers end very quickly as a result of bad decisions. I followed my gut and relied on two of the five Cs of credit: Character and Capacity. Character meant that a customer would make his loan payments before buying food for his family; Capacity meant he had sufficient financial assets to make adjustments when necessary.

Then I met Joe Pepitone, the Yankee first baseman. One of my customers was related to Joe and he walked into my office one day with Joe at his side. Other customers saw him, and in a matter of minutes the bank was packed with every kid in the neighborhood, looking to shake his hand and get an autograph. Joe's image was one of a very talented baseball player. He was also well known for his "off the field" activities, and at age 25 I wanted to be a part of his entourage. During the next several months I was part of Joe's crowd, until he didn't show up for a game after a night of partying. He was fired the next day, and within weeks signed with a team in Japan. I followed his career, on and off the field, for the next year until he returned to the States.

This was the first time in my life that I started to build confidence in my abilities as a banker. I could open any door and "sell the bank" to just about anybody. I had established credibility in the Bay Ridge community. Mom's reaction was expected: "They don't know you like I do," she said. I brushed the comment aside and came to the realization that my communication skills had been developed as a small boy who had to be his mother's ears. What I had thought of as an albatross had actually given me a talent that would carry me through a banking career that lasted more than 40 years. When little else was going right in my personal life, I could put it aside during working hours, during which I was respected, well treated, and genuinely good at my job.

My social life also started to develop at that time. When my marriage to Betty came to an end in 1969, I had developed friends through banking that couldn't do enough to help out. My associates and supervisors at Bankers Trust also knew my value and worked with me. But the financial pressures of the divorce led me to accept a position at another bank—a big mistake. From day one it was apparent they didn't care about my personal problems, and within two years I ate some pride and went back to Bankers Trust, where I stayed until the bank was sold in the late 1970s.

Looking Stylish, 1946

CHAPTER

10

The circle of friends that I developed during 1969 and 1970 centered around the various night spots where I spent most Friday and Saturday nights. I started to date and soon learned that the late '60s were very different from the early part of the decade. If you were inclined to, you could spend every night with a different woman. The Sexual Revolution was in full swing, and I climbed aboard for the ride. I partied hard for the next year, but ultimately found this new life a bit boring, and most certainly "plastic." It wasn't real and I wanted so much to settle down and be a father and husband in a stable loving environment.

I decided to drop by one of the clubs on a week-night, something I rarely did, but I was on vacation and had little money to do anything else. As I walked into the lobby my eye caught a glimpse of a young, dark-haired girl—yes, I mean girl—sitting by herself watching the main entrance. She was apparently waiting for someone. I walked by and didn't give it another thought until I left several hours later, and saw her sitting in the same spot. I casually asked, "Is anyone worth waiting for this long?" She replied, "Apparently not," and we continued talking. Her name was Chris and within 18 months she would be my second wife.

At 19 she was almost eight years younger than me, and we made a date for the following week. I remember picking her up on date night. I rang the doorbell and she came out almost immediately, a surprise, since I was usually invited in to meet the parents. After the second date she admitted to living alone in a furnished room, and I found myself wanting to care for this young but apparently gutsy lady. There were family issues, she told me, which had caused her to move out on her own. Her family was old-school Greek Cypriot, and she was fighting the old ways in this country where freedom meant so much more than it did in her parents' native land.

Her father, in fact, had found his own freedom and was living with a new family in Arizona, leaving behind Chris' mother and the house they had bought soon after coming to the United States. I felt reasonably comfortable with the European mentality and customs, which I found similar to my own Italian culture. But Chris was one of six children and only her younger sister still lived at home. Were they all running away from something, and if so, what? That question never crossed my mind then, but time would again teach me that it was something I should have asked early on.

From the outset I was treated well, even when the family was told I had been married before and had two daughters. Being accepted was a priority in my business life, and that same attribute in my private life was important to me. As a result, I missed the not-so-subtle signals that should have forewarned me of things to come. I wanted to prove to the world that the breakup of my first marriage was only one misstep in life, and that I was ultimately capable of cultivating a sound family environment, as a husband and father. I would find out too late that you carry the scars of your youth, forever. If you are trying to distance yourself from a bad environment, you need to make sure that you aren't heading in a direction where you will repeat the same mistakes.

Within a couple of years we had married, bought a home on Long Island, and started a family. I was commuting to the City to work every day, and commuting to Staten Island on weekends to exercise my visitation with Dawn and Denise. I brought them out for overnight stays and holidays. Over time, the stress of work and financial problems caused a drop in those visits from biweekly to monthly. I always felt a deep sense of guilt in my inability to see them more often and do more for them, but now I had a son, and the job of balancing work, family and finances became a full-time job.

My Dad was now residing in a nursing home on Staten Island, and my mothers' demands for support continued to rise. Who else could she turn to? Her sister Sylvia was the only family member other than me that tried to help her as often as possible. This is the same person who came to my rescue after the breakup of my first marriage. Very few people visited my Dad at the nursing home. Mom had another sister and a brother, but they had no interest in visiting the institution where Dad was "existing." Their children, my cousins, were also among the missing. I always thought they loved their uncle. I guess they found it difficult watching him deteriorate over time. It's a reminder of what's to come for all of us eventually, a debilitating illness and a slow journey toward death. I remember challenging one of my cousins regarding his decision not to visit my Dad. He veiled his guilt in a defensive tirade about his desire to remember his uncle in better times, when he could walk and talk. He went on to condemn our decision to allow the brain surgery that ultimately resulted in such massive damage. I bit my tongue, but didn't remind him that his father had blessed the surgery, because without it my Dad would have had only weeks to live.

I was angry and disappointed in the family members who had abandoned a sweet, considerate man who had become a reminder of their own mortality. Mom and I did as much as we could until the stress forced us to consider some remedies to offset the hours of driving several times a week. Mom was living on Staten Island, while I lived in South Farmingdale with Chris and Ed Jr. Dawn and Denise lived with their mother on Staten Island. I was the mouse in the maze trying to navigate through it all, and work at the same time. Something had to be done.

CHAPTER

11

It was during one of those visits to the nursing home that the subject of moving Dad to a Long Island facility first came up. Mom had suggested that she move in with us, but the idea was a non-starter, at least with me. A half step toward living under the same roof was purchasing a two-family house where we could all live in close proximity to Dad's nursing home. It would eliminate a ton of driving, and I could use the re-captured hours being a husband and father. It all made so much sense, especially when Mom offered to offset the cost of a larger home with a gift of cash towards the purchase. There's nothing like money to transform a bad idea into a great one.

We found a builder through a local realtor and purchased the land in East Meadow and construction of a mother/daughter high ranch began almost immediately. I should have realized that this mother/daughter was actually going to be a mother/son—with a wife the mother never liked. A bad combination under any set of circumstances. Our old house in South Farmingdale sold in a heartbeat, and we all moved into the new place just before Christmas of 1976. The novelty of owning a brand new home wore off quickly. Within 48 hours, as I remember it. It was on Christmas morning that I awoke to a voice and an image at the foot of our bed. It was Mom, rollers in her hair, without makeup and apparently very angry at something. I was trying to emerge from the fog of sleep, and make sense of just what possibly could be so wrong.

While I was trying to decipher Mom's reason for entering our room, Chris was screaming in my other ear. Clearly Mom had made a fatal mistake of invading our bedroom at 6 a.m. to advise us that she was cold. Ultimately I found the new oil burner doing absolutely nothing, although it was 19 degrees. I tried to contact the builder, but was advised that he had just left for Costa Rica. "When will he be back?" The phone went dead. I lit a fire in the living room fireplace, and started to call the local oil burner service technicians in the neighborhood. I finally found one willing to make the house call on Christmas morning after I mentioned that we had a young son and an aging grandmother living with us. The serviceman admitted that, being Jewish, he had nothing better to do on Christmas morning. Still, Christmas was Christmas, so it would cost double.

With the heat restored, we tried to enjoy the holiday, but I knew that we had to establish some ground rules if this new arrangement was to work. Mom had her own apartment on the first floor of the house and a private entrance at the back. She had access to our part of the house through a connecting door that opened into the den and the staircase to our space upstairs. We had discussed the space allocation in great detail prior to the beginning of construction. Now that we had moved in, Mom had other ideas. She wanted access to the den as part of her space. She also wanted to use the front door to come and go. She felt that she had the right to access any part of the house at any time. Why did she feel this way? The money that she contributed towards the construction gave her the right. Needless to say, we didn't agree with her, and the future suddenly looked as bleak as the cloudy winter sky.

We made it through the holidays that year by virtue of little Ed and Dawn and Denise who were with us for several days during Christmas recess. The joy in their faces as they opened their gifts, the fun they had with their just-unwrapped toys and the impromptu fashion show as they tried on their new clothes lightened the mood. When it was time to take them home, I packed the car with their gifts, put the girls in the back seat and made the trip back to their mother on Staten Island. The trip was filled with conversation about the good times spent with Dad—and Chris, who always tried to do the right thing when it came to the kids. She felt genuine affection for them and never showed any favoritism towards her own blood child. My mother tried to treat them all the same, but it became apparent to me, and later on to them, that "Nani" did indeed have a favorite, and that was Dawn.

The trip back from Staten Island was always a sad one for me. I missed the girls from the minute I dropped them off, and never knew what I was going to find when I arrived back at home. Mom would do her best to discredit Chris at every opportunity. We tried to eat a few meals a week together, although there was always criticism or a face showing her dissatisfaction with Chris' cooking. Mom was as obvious as she was with the class system she had created for the kids.

We made it through the start of the New Year without too many problems with Mom, but moving Dad to a nursing home near our new home had taken its toll on him. The change in surroundings and a new daily routine resulted in constant little illnesses. We brought little Ed to visit on a regular basis, and Dad beamed when we put his grandson next to him in the hospital bed so they could share a box of animal crackers. Eddie Jr. would put the cookies into Dad's mouth one at a time. The little guy actually seemed to know that his grandfather wasn't well and wouldn't be around much longer.

It was late in January 1977 when Dad suddenly went into a coma. Mom was apparently upset by the sudden deterioration, and of course she took it out on those around her. She seemed to forget that I was equally frightened about the impending loss of my father. As usual, it was all about her. For the next several weeks I visited him daily on my way home from work, then drove back to the nursing home after dinner with Mom. After about three weeks the intravenous feeding caused a reaction, and dark purple patches started to erupt on his arms, legs and body. Dr. Colletti came into Dad's room during one of my visits and explained that the IV would be terminated because of this sudden allergic reaction. I was assured that Dad felt no pain, and was resting comfortably deep within the coma. The doctor went on to explain that he would inject fluids into Dad's muscle tissue to prevent dehydration, which would be a painful death. I looked directly into the doctor's eyes and reminded him of his earlier comment that Dad felt nothing and asked that he dispense with the fluid injections. "Just make him comfortable doctor. No more needles or procedures at this point. I want him to leave this world with a little dignity." The doctor nodded, and for the next few days we sat next to Dad's bed and waited.

It was Saturday, Feb. 26, 1977. Chris and I were busy getting ready for a wedding we'd been invited to on Sunday. That meant a trip to the barber for me, the hairdresser for her, getting my suit from the cleaners, ironing a shirt and picking out a tie. Mom would baby-sit young Ed, and Chris and I would try to have a little time away from the house, the nursing home and Mom, who would enjoy spending time with her grandson. After dinner that night I felt the urge to visit Dad, and drove to the nursing home around nine-thirty. His eyes were closed, and I sat next to his bed and watched his chest moving up and down with each breath. I got up from my chair after what seemed like a half hour and walked to the window to look out onto Front Street. All of a sudden I heard a voice call out, "Edward, is that you?" The voice was my father's. I turned and said, "Dad you're awake. You've been sleeping for weeks." He didn't answer me, but followed my movements back to the side of the bed. I told him I'd be right back and went out to the nurses' station to tell the staff. "My Dad is awake. He opened his eyes, and called my name." The nurses looked at each other and followed me back to his room. He was sleeping again. The nurse explained that it happens occasionally with coma cases: They awaken for a few brief seconds and then regress again into a deep sleep. I drove home feeling uplifted that just maybe there was a chance he might recover.

I slept well that night knowing that Dad had at least recognized me for a few fleeting seconds. The next morning, Mom went to visit him with some friends. I never got to tell her about my experience with Dad the night before. She assured me that she would be back early so we could leave for the wedding. I had just showered and shaved when the phone rang. "Edward, this is Peg. I am at the nursing home with your Mom. You'd better get here quick—your Dad just passed away." I overheard Mom in the background. "He should have been here with me, not going to some damned wedding when his father is on his death bed. I need his support. I just lost my husband." I hung up the phone and mumbled, "Yeah, Mom, and I just lost my Dad. But as usual, it's always about you."

I walked into Dad's room oblivious to who was there. I wanted to focus on him right now. Mom started to speak and I glared at her and yelled, "Not now." Dad's eyes seemed to be gazing out the window that I had been looking out of the night before. I touched his hand, then his forehead and it felt slightly warm. I had so little experience with death. My family had only buried one person and that was my grandfather. I wasn't frightened by the sight of my father's lifeless body, but I did feel anger that this sweet man never really did much in his life other than work and try to make his wife happy. That and a few short trips to the Catskills, where he was berated for eating too much. A new '56 Chevy that got "better care and more attention than his wife did," as my mother complained. Now he was free from his illness, the paralysis and her. I found myself closing his eyes with my index finger as Mom, her friends and the nurses looked on. I found the chapel and had long cry. I wanted to be alone and through my thoughts communicate with the man that I never got to spend much time with. Because I had never belonged to him, only to her.

The next few days after Dad's passing were filled with making funeral arrangements, then enduring a wake that lasted three days. I argued with Mom over the need for a casket, because Dad had always said he wanted to be cremated. He was as claustrophobic as I am, and any thought of being stored away for eternity in a box buried under six feet of dirt was enough to cause a panic attack. But Mom also wanted to dispense with purchasing a new suit, shirt and tie for the viewing. "It will be burned to ashes, too," she noted. "A total waste of money." I reminded her that Dad always joked about being laid out in a tux, having worn one only once in his 68 years, the day he married Mom on August 24th, 1940. He referred to that day as "the happiest day of my life." I assume he meant that one day.

I remember as a small boy being told the story of their wedding. Mom's father, my grandfather, did not attend the weddings of any of his children. His reason was simple: He didn't approve of their choices of life partners. He was an absolute ruler, and defying him always brought severe retribution. Does any of this sound familiar? I guess the apple really doesn't fall too far from the tree. Grandpa's traits were clearly visible in two of his four children, my mother and her brother, Tom. The other two sisters were more in the mold of my grandmother. Sometimes I actually wished I was born to one of them.

I ultimately prevailed, and Dad was laid out in a new blue suit, complete with a new shirt and tie. The funeral director had pointed out that Dad had lost so much weight over the years that his old clothes would look terrible. We selected a cloth-covered grey coffin, the least expensive one available. Dad's wake became an instant pulpit for Mom. "It was so hard for me to take care of him all those years. I am deaf and needed support from my "only child." If I had a daughter things would have been different. Now Angelo will rest in peace and maybe I can have some kind of a life." I heard this litany throughout the wake and the funeral for the next three days, and I never saw her cry during that time.

Family members who meant well reminded me of my responsibility toward my mother now that Dad was gone. At the restaurant after the funeral was over, I endured more of the same from Moms' friends who were still amazed by her accomplishments as a deaf woman. My cousins started to giggle when they heard me blurt out, "Move over Pop, I'm jumping in there with you." They were finally beginning to understand that it wasn't easy being me.

Chris and I along with Mom retreated back to the house with some of the family where the advice and lectures went on for several more hours. I was numb at this point, and felt hopelessly trapped. I listened and nodded, and was relieved when they all left. I locked the door behind them and went to bed.

Grandpa Natoli and King, 1948

CHAPTER

12

I returned to work the following week. It was difficult to concentrate on work with the knowledge that Mom would find some way to anger Chris while I was at the office. I didn't have to wait too long for the situation to erupt. Each day I received a full report when I walked in the front door. First it was Chris and later in the evening it was Mom's turn to bitch. The connecting door became the main topic of discussion, and after a really bad confrontation, Mom went to visit her sister Cathy out in Coram for a few days.

When she returned several days later, I had closed up the doorway and converted it to an extra closet on Mom's side. It wasn't done as an act of cruelty, but Chris and I were going through some tough times, and the constant problem caused by Mom's easy access to our living space was only making things worse. Over time, I would learn that our marriage would ultimately come to an abrupt end despite the remedies that I put in place to keep Mom and Chris from fighting.

Mom entered her apartment through the back door, and in a matter of five minutes she opened the connecting door to access our part of the house. In an instant she lost her temper and started pounding on the new wall that now blocked her access. Three weeks later she told me she was moving into an apartment in Brooklyn across the street from some old friends who really loved her and appreciated her in every way. I saw it as the only solution to a bad situation, and promised to return the money she had given us when we built the house, in which she was supposed to live rent-free for the rest of her life. Little did I know that when Chris and I separated years later, the legal system would not recognize the debt. The courts looked at it as a gift.

Throughout my life, my mother was generous. The problem was the price tag that was placed on each act of generosity. I never asked for her help. She would always offer it at a time when we were getting along. I repeated the same mistake a number of times and ultimately made a decision to respectfully decline her help, no matter how dire the circumstances became.

With Mom out of the house and out of our lives for awhile, Chris and I tried to settle into a normal routine, and within two months she became pregnant with our second child. Nicolle was born on January 19th, 1978. The new baby allowed us to focus our attention on the kids, and my older daughters doted on their new baby sister whenever they came out to Long Island for a visit. Over time, I resumed communication with Mom, and she focused most of her attention on the kids when she visited, but the old anger was still evident between her and Chris. During Mom's visits she would now complain about her friends back in Brooklyn. "They talked me into moving back there, and now they act like they want nothing to do with me," she told us. It became apparent that no one could live up to Mom's expectations for very long. The old expression about familiarity breeding contempt was dead-on when it came to my mother. The best way to cope with Mom was to accept her in small doses, and schedule visits interspaced with long periods of no contact.

The Blizzard of '78 hit the Northeast hard and closed down most of Long Island for weeks. My commute from East Meadow to Maspeth, Queens was a pain in the butt in good weather, but became completely insane in bad weather. In those days, the bosses seldom declared a "banking holiday," so if you worked for a bank you found a way to get to work. The initial forecast of 18 inches or more was enough to convince me to pack a bag with extra clothes and prepare to stay in Queens for several nights. When I arrived at work on the morning of the storm, I contacted a local motel popular with over-the-road truck drivers, and booked a room. I could easily walk the two blocks to the motel and back to the bank in the morning. I stocked the refrigerator at the bank with enough provisions to ensure that I'd have something to eat and drink for a few days.

I sat at my desk and gazed out the window. Several inches of snow had accumulated in the past two hours, and it was getting heavier by the minute. The ringing of the phone brought me back from the hypnotic effect of the falling snow. It was Chris, who was in a state of panic. "The baby is sick and I have no way of getting to the drug store," she informed me. "You have to come home right after work." Nicole was a month old and Eddie Jr. was three and a half. I had made sure Chris had everything she would need before I left for the office that morning, and found myself getting angry with her. My job was the only thing that held us all together. I was paying alimony and child support to my first wife, and actually worked a part time job to supplement my pay from the bank. I couldn't just pick up and head home in the middle of the day. I tried to settle her down, and called our local pharmacy to ask them to deliver a bottle of Triaminic Syrup. The baby had a mild cold, but Chris was acting like she was suffering from an illness that could be fatal. Why was she acting this way?

Chris and I had been meeting with a psychologist on a weekly basis for the past year. We both carried the scars of a less-than-normal childhood, which made it all the more difficult to cope with the pressures of a marriage and children. We also had to cope with two children from my prior marriage, and then, of course, my mother. During the past year and a half intimacy had all but stopped and frustration had set in. Maybe Dr. Ray could help.

I dialed his number and he picked up on the first ring. He had already gotten a call from Chris. I explained my situation and asked if he could try to settle her down. It was now early afternoon and the snow was piling up. The news channels were reporting hundreds of accidents on slick roads and were urging everyone to stay put. An hour later, the doctor called me back and seriously advised me to get home regardless of the danger.

He was deeply concerned for Chris and the children. He thought she might be suffering from post-partum depression. At three o'clock I locked the doors at the bank, sent the staff home and climbed into my car for the trek to Long Island. Door-to-door the trip was just over 20 miles, but two hours later I was still six miles from home on the Northern State Parkway. The CB radio started to crackle, and I heard a voice of panic from a motorist several miles ahead of me, "There's no way off this parkway," he said. "All the exit ramps have over 15 inches of snow, if you can see them at all."

I knew I had to get off the parkway at all costs. The blizzard was intensifying and visibility was extremely poor. I saw an exit sign and followed the tail lights of the car in front of me and prayed. At the bottom of the exit ramp I realized I was at the intersection of Jericho Turnpike and Glen Cove Road. These were two of the busiest commercial streets in Nassau County, and the plows had already been through at least one time. I headed south on Glen Cove Road and made a left turn onto Stewart Avenue in Garden City and found myself directly behind a snow plow that was headed east. I made up my mind to follow that plow as long as it was headed in the general direction of my home. The voice on the CB mentioned something about hundreds of cars that were stranded on the parkway that I'd exited not too long ago. Cell phones or "portable phones" as they were called back then were only for the very rich. The CB radio was the only form of communication in a bad situation. I was headed home but couldn't relay that fact to Chris. I continued to follow the plow east on Stewart Avenue. At the Merrick Avenue intersection, I had to make a choice. I could try to navigate through Eisenhower Park or make a right turn on Merrick Avenue for the last two miles to my house. The plow made the decision for me. He turned right and I followed him. At Front Street, I turned left for the last three blocks to Maple Avenue where I lived. I tried to build up as much speed as possible in the hope that I could make it to my driveway, but the snow was so deep that I aimed for a snow bank. The front wheels of the car were a foot higher than the rear, and that's where the car stayed for the next two days, four houses away from home.

I opened the front door and stepped into the warm safety of home. Chris had built a fire and was seated on the floor playing with Nicolle and Eddie. This was not the same woman that was falling apart four hours earlier. She was calm and paid little attention to me. She never even considered the possible consequences of demanding that I get home that day. People were stranded in their cars for the next several days, and I could have been one of them. Her complete recovery over a four hour period was something I would never forget, or forgive.

The banks were closed for the next few days, and I was able to dig out the car and finally get it back into my driveway. I was chatting with the next-door neighbor during a break in the shoveling when Chris came to the window and asked me to come into the house. The neighbor looked up at Chris, who turned quickly away without acknowledgement. I apologized for my wife's behavior and explained that our baby was ill and that my wife was extremely worried. But as I walked to my front door I remembered similar incidents in our old neighborhood. It seemed Chris would look for any reason to terminate my conversations with neighbors, and it was always when I was talking to a woman.

I stepped into the house, stomped the snow from my boots and asked her what she wanted. She seemed to be searching for an answer, and finally asked when I would start clearing off the back deck. "Is that why you interrupted my conversation with our new neighbor? My God, you didn't even say hello or introduce yourself," I said. She never answered me and returned to the kitchen.

CHAPTER

13

The next few years were filled with countless sessions with Dr. Ray. It was clear that Chris and I were growing further apart, and I was obsessed with making the marriage work. Or was I afraid of having a second marriage fail? In the eyes of family and friends, it would certainly prove that I was the problem, someone who should never have married again. There are two more children to care for. He will be paying for the rest of his life.

I couldn't argue with these assessments, because they were to some degree correct.

I wanted to avoid throwing blame at Chris because I knew from the beginning that she had been traumatized by her father, just as her older sister had been. Chris' oldest brother intervened and enrolled his sister at a university where she would live on campus, and not be a target of the father's assaults. The one thing he didn't count on was the availability of two other young sisters that still lived at home. As I mentioned previously, "dear old Dad" left for Arizona with his new wife one day, and ultimately fathered another daughter. I met him once years later when he briefly came back to New York, and actually visited his two young-est daughters.

Chris had described him as a tall well built-man, but the guy I met barely matched my five-foot-eight inches in height and was skinny as a rail with a bad smoker's cough that would kill him two years later. In Chris' eyes as a young girl, she saw this man very differently. And, of course, fear changes perspective.

From my earliest days with Chris, I used denial to brush aside the signals that should have convinced me to re-evaluate our relationship. We had broken off several times, only to get back together soon after. The sessions with Dr. Ray became more frequent as our relationship deteriorated to the point where I started looking elsewhere for love, affection and understanding. I was torn between calling it quits and staying the course for the benefit of Ed Jr. and Nicolle, whom I adored. I already had two older daughters that had gone through a marriage breakup. How would they view their Dad if it happened again? How would I explain it? Could I handle another failure? And then there was Mom. She would be thrilled. She had told me not to marry again. As usual, I hadn't listened.

My obsession with getting away from Mom sent me in the wrong direction time after time. If you're constantly looking over your shoulder, it's hard to evaluate where you're heading. In my case, it resulted in two failed marriages. On the bright side, I had four wonderful children that would be mine, forever. I had reached the end of my rope, and on a Saturday morning in February 1983, I made my decision.

I was sitting at the breakfast table looking out the sliding glass doors at the big tree in the yard. It was covered with snow on a cold, gray winter morning. Chris was sitting across from me, and when there was conversation it focused on what was wrong with the house, the furniture, the car, or her life as a mother and wife. Nothing was ever "right." I had tried to set her up with a booth in a flea market, selling little trinkets that were manufactured by one of my clients. I literally told everyone in the neighborhood about it in the hope that they would stop by and maybe buy something. I wanted to boost her self-image. Unfortunately, I had to bring her there, set up her tables and displays, care for the children the rest of the day, cook, pick her up later in the day and then come home and get the kids fed, bathed and ready for bed. This went on for several weekends, and ended in a tirade of complaints about the merchandise, the location of her tables etc. Her little business closed down and I was relieved.

I casually asked Chris about her latest session with Dr. Ray. She looked at me and told me that she wasn't going back for any more. In a rare moment of strength and conviction, she said: "I am what I am. I have no desire to change, and if that's a problem for you, maybe we should get a divorce." I never answered her. The next day I called an attorney and made an appointment to consult with him the following day. Chris joined me for that initial talk and agreed to the loose structure of a separation agreement that would be incorporated into our divorce decree. I agreed to move out of the house as soon as I found a suitable apartment.

I felt relieved despite the financial and emotional strain it placed on me, and the children would no longer sense the tension and distance that had driven their mother and me to a place that we could never return from. I knew at that time that I wasn't running away from life, but merely repeating the same mistakes over and over again.

During the time that we had left together, I focused on the kids. I loved feeding Nicolle as a baby and still enjoyed the little naps that we took together on the couch. She would lie on my chest, and the beating of my heart would lull her to sleep. I also like to play the Bette Midler recording of "The Rose" at nap time. I remember these times in particular because we would not experience that closeness again for many years to come. Nicolle was indeed my little rose, with a quiet undemanding personality. Those traits would result in her being overlooked because as we all know, "the squeaky wheel gets the grease."

Ed Jr. was another story. He was always extremely active and we didn't realize that the abundance of apple juice that he craved was, in fact, not good for him. He was on a sugar high until he was 10 or 11. I can't remember a time when he would sit quietly and read or play. When he was about two, he liked to crawl up behind our tri-color Collie, grab the poor dog by the testicles and hold on for the ride as Ringo tried to escape. The dog would run from room to room with Eddie along for the ride. If he was watching TV, he was always acting out the role of the superhero. If he was in the backyard pool by himself, the water resembled a wave pool that was occupied by a dozen other kids. It was amusing to a point, but his energy level would pose some problems when he went to school.

As I moved out of the house on Feb. 23, 1983, I tried to cling to those special memories, as I did with Dawn and Denise back in 1969. I found myself thinking about the house on East 52nd Street in Brooklyn, and the spare bedroom that was outfitted with a complete play kitchen for Dawn when she was only two, and our dog Frisky, who never suffered as Ringo did.

Then there was the panic when Dawn ate the contents of an ashtray. Poison Control assured us that she would be fine—and likely never take up smoking. They were right.

Denise was only a week or two old when her mother and I separated. Trying to get to know her from afar was so difficult. It was her mother who took care of her during the times when she suffered from constant and painful ear infections. Denise had come into the world as a "preemie," and stayed at the hospital for weeks after her mother had been sent home. The doctor had miscalculated her due date, and when Denise was born through caesarian section—as was Dawn— she weighed in well under five pounds. She had ear and vision problems from the outset, and I can clearly remember her telling anyone who looked into her eyes, "I am cross-eyed." Despite her size at birth, she had a strong personality and would defy us until we ultimately gave in to her whims.

These four children of two different mothers ultimately grew close over the years, and they would also welcome another child into their group in the future. I am still amazed at their sense of love for each other. They all had some missing pieces in their lives through no fault of their own, but never abandoned the hope for better times and a deep sense of love for each other. There was a common ground in each of their lives.

I take little credit for their development, because I was always considered the cause of whatever went wrong in their lives. It was easy to blame Dad, who was always busy with something, or someone, else. Divorce in those days resulted in the children being, in effect, the sole property of the custodial parent, which was, and is, almost always the mother. Dad's primary responsibility was financial: "You have to pay for your freedom, Ed." I accepted that responsibility and lived up to it. I never missed an alimony or child support check. I paid for pre-school and whatever else was needed. Need was determined by the custodial parent and the court system always considered the needs of the children first. All Dad could do was comply.

I'm OK with all of that, but in the first few months after Chris and I separated, I struggled just to exist. Yes, I had that little house in the Poconos near the slopes of Camelback, but I had to rent it out to weekend skiers just to cover the bills on the place.

The banking industry in that era seriously frowned on their employees doing any kind of part time work. Those bastards actually believed that you could live well on what they paid each week. They also felt that any outside influence would be reflected in your work ethic and productivity. That was all bullshit, really. They just wanted to own an individual, lock, stock and barrel. While I totally enjoyed my 40-plus years as a banker, I couldn't make it on what I earned back then, and had no choice but to find additional sources of income. My "superiors," as they were called back then, could easily prey on someone who was enduring financial hardship. They knew that you needed your job and couldn't afford to be out of work. That meant a smaller piece of the pie at raise time, and there was little you could do about it. After all, they were your "superiors," and therefore they always did the right thing. I learned from those times, and preached to every one of my kids never to share their personal life or financial situation with the boss or co-workers. And never tell the boss that you need your job or need to work. In the eyes of corporate America, it's a sign of weakness, and weakness could always be exploited.

Mom, Dad, and me at the Niagara Falls, 1949

CHAPTER

14

It was just days away from my 40th birthday. It was a rainy Friday night, and I was alone in that sparsely furnished apartment. The ski season was winding down in the Pocono's, and very few rentals were available during the late winter and early spring. The apartment was rented to me through a banking contract at a lower than market rate, just to help me out until I got back on solid ground. I wanted no part of being obligated to anyone. That practice had never worked in the past. Through tears of frustration, fear and loneliness, I made a decision to choose a new path. From that point on, things would be different. I had spent the first 40 years of my life making mistakes because I always thought that I needed the approval of other people. It was time to learn from those past mistakes, and never repeat them. I had told my personal business to anyone who would listen, and that worked against me. Why did I constantly look for justification from others? I had already done enough of that, with bad results. In the future, I'd make decisions that were right for me, not to gain acceptance from family and friends who had made as many, if not more, mistakes than I had.

I spent that weekend building that kitchen table I needed. I bought 2X10 pine boards and bolted them together with slats on the underside. The boards had been planed smooth and only needed a little sanding. I applied coat after coat of polyurethane, and sanded again after each coat. Finally, it was ready for the legs, and I purchased four sturdy chrome jobs and mounted them to the underside. I opened a folding chair and sat at the table for the first time on Sunday night. It looked beautiful, and I made a mental note to purchase four wicker-and-chrome chairs to finish off my new kitchen set when I could afford them. I had made it through another solitary weekend by keeping my mind and body occupied. I felt good about my accomplishment. Just then the doorbell rang.

I looked out my front window and saw Chris standing at my front door. Until this day I wonder why I answered it. She certainly hadn't dropped by to wish me well in my new "home." Maybe she had brought me a little housewarming gift? Did she have a change of heart and want me back? Then I thought about the little ones and rushed to open the door. There was no "hello" or "how are you?" She pushed past me and ran up the stairs. I followed and asked, no yelled, what the hell are you doing? She went from room to room, all three of them, and into the bathroom where she pushed the shower curtain aside. She started to head for my closet in the bedroom and at that point I blocked her way. She finally blurted out the words, "Where is she?"

Chris was sure I left her for another woman, just as her father had left her mother many years before. I felt the need to convince her that I had no one concealed in the closet, and opened each door to reveal nothing but clothes, shoes and an ironing board. Why did I feel the need to do that? I had lived as a celibate for a long time with her and would have had every right to a relationship. She walked down the stairs and left, but not before telling me. "I have one mission in life, and that's to make your life miserable from now on."

In the coming weeks, I worked days at the bank, and spent several evenings a week providing business and financial advice to clients that were referred to me by my attorney. Even he had an ulterior motive. He wanted me to generate additional income to pay the legal fees. Things were looking up despite the constant calls from Chris or my attorney with a list of the latest complaints and demands. I took it all in stride and got more deeply involved in my career, and my new "consulting business." Within a few months I asked my secretary out on a dinner date. OK, I still made a few mistakes.

Deb was 26 and I was 40. She had never been married before and lived with her mom in an apartment on the south shore of Nassau County. She had become my friend and confidant during the past few months and I shared a lot with her. One day at lunch, a popular song about a guy and his secretary was playing in the background. One of the verses in the song "Take a Letter Maria" was "Would you like to have dinner tonight?"

Hey there's an idea. Let's get involved with someone from the workplace and really screw things up. After several dates, it was apparent she wanted things in life that I could not offer, even if I wanted to. The relationship started with all the passion and euphoria I could want, but the downside was revealed by terrible mood swings and a pretty bad temper. I had reacted to an attractive woman who seemed to care for me, and pushed aside all the signals that pointed towards failure again.

I broke it off soon after, and she requested a transfer to another department in the bank, but not without telling the HR director that we had been involved for several months. He was also going through a divorce and probably sleeping with his secretary, so he found a way to calm things down. Yes, I had made a mistake from the beginning with this woman. I was trying to recapture my youth without any regard for someone who wanted all the things that I already had. The bright side of the equation showed that I was beginning to recognize my errors in judgment before things got out of hand.

I came to the conclusion that I couldn't get involved with anyone until I first learned to live with, and by, myself. During the spring of 1983, I took frequent drives up to the Pocono house on weekends when it wasn't rented. I had won a Grumman aluminum canoe at a golf outing and strapped it to the roof of my car. The house was on a small lake and I liked to fish. It was quiet and peaceful. A business associate turned friend—and now a client of my consulting business—had built a chalet on the adjoining property, so I very often combined those weekends with business. I brought a few books, my guitar and some sheet music and enough food and liquor for the weekend. I barbecued a steak that first night, had a few drinks, watched the sun set, and then watched TV until I dozed off.

The next morning I awoke to the sounds of birds and nothing else. I had slept better than I had in months. I started the coffee and took a cup outside. I sat on the little porch and took in the lake and the wildlife. I took my second cup down to the canoe, pushed off the bank and floated aimlessly around the lake. My mind was always racing back on Long Island, but this environment was therapeutic at this point in my life. I spent the rest of the day cutting steps into the slope that led down to the waters edge, used my chain saw to cut the railroad ties that would be the steps, and hammered pieces of steel rebar into the ground to anchor them in place. I admired my work and realized that this was the kind of mindless activity that could help me escape reality for days at a time. It also renewed or charged my battery for what was to come the following week.

That night, I drove into Mount Pocono for dinner. I drove down Route 940 and made a left turn on Route 611, about a half mile to a little restaurant named The Country Breadboard. I walked in, past the bakery counter filled with fresh breads and rolls and cakes, and asked to be seated in the dining room.

"How many in your party sir? Just me, I replied. "All of our small tables are filled right now. Please have a seat out on the patio, and we should be able to seat you in about 20 minutes." Can I get a Scotch delivered out there? "Of course, what would you like"? Dewars on the rocks!

I walked outside where a group of 20 or so other diners were also waiting for tables. Family groups of four to six, several couples, and then there was me. I thought of a Neal Diamond song and the lyric, "I never cared for the sound of being alone." It was time to learn.

I sipped my drink and watched the other groups. Was I meant to live the rest of my life alone? I did have four wonderful children from my two previous marriages. Betty and I had settled into a relatively smooth relationship. We really never had a chance from the beginning. I had gone through a period of time when I criticized her mothering techniques. I got angry with myself because I sounded so much like my mother at times. Dawn and Denise commented at dinner one night that their mom bought boxes of Weaver chicken at the supermarket and they loved it. The math proved that you could buy two or three whole chickens for the same price and cook several meals. But why was my way the right way? I was sipping a five dollar scotch while I waited for my table at the restaurant. I could have had a soda for a buck. To achieve any changes in my life, I would have to be tolerant of other people, and cease the endless criticism that I had learned to live with.

My dinner consisted of batter fried chicken and fries that night. I drank a beer with my meal, and when I paid the check I noticed that my dinner would have cost eight dollars less if I dispensed with the scotch and the beer. Money was a dominating factor at that time, because it was tied to the obligations that I had put on myself. It was never about accumulating wealth. Unfortunately, alimony and child support payments consumed most of my income, and without the "side" money I wouldn't have made it through those years. That same situation really impacted the time I had left for the kids.

CHAPTER

15

The rest of that first spring and summer after Chris and I separated was filled with work, more work, meetings with my attorney to hammer out a separation agreement and constant phone calls to advise me of what I was guilty of in Chris' eyes.

My sanity was regained on the weekends in Pennsylvania, and coaching little Ed's soccer team. I enrolled him at five in an attempt to channel his energy into a sport that involved so much physical activity that I got tired just watching him. The local soccer league turned us down at first because the minimum age was set at six. They would however allow him to play if I agreed to coach. I accepted and learned the basics of the game from an experienced coach and the rules from a book.

This was the first time I really concentrated on other parents, and quickly found out that they all had problems, too. Most overcame them because of the bigger picture. No one was perfect and the key to any relationship required respect, understanding and tolerance. Did the good outweigh the bad? I was amazed that 90 percent of the kids had just one parent at the games, and none of them would stay at the field to watch a practice. The mothers would drop the kids off, and take off to do whatever they did for the next hour and a half. I had become a babysitter, but really enjoyed working with my own son and his teammates. There were too many times when the parents didn't get back on time. Ed and I would have to hang out with the other kids until their parents returned with apologies and reasons for the delay.

My role as coach for Ed's soccer team became the conduit for the next stage in my life. Little Michael was the most talented kid that I coached. He had speed, mobility and could kick the ball the entire length of the field at nine. He only lacked the tenacity and aggression that would make him a complete player for his age group. I was in my third year with the league and had never seen his dad at a game or practice. It was his mother Barbara that attended every event. One day I asked her if her husband could try to attend a game because Michael was really good at soccer and his dad's presence might bolster his confidence. The following Saturday, both parents came to watch Michael play. He rushed over to me and pointed to his parents. His eyes lit up when he said. "Coach, my Dad is here to watch me play." The transformation was unbelievable. That little guy played his heart out and scored several times. Later, he would join the travel team as one of the elite players.

Yes, it was OK in those days for some kids to be better than others in sports. Unlike today, when all kids are winners, and there are no losers. But that's the topic of another book.

I also took something away from the field that day: a clear example of the importance of bonding with each child regardless of the activity. Something as simple as helping them with homework, attending their athletic events, school related events, or just talking with them. I would find out that this process is not easy to achieve if both parents aren't committed to it. During the remainder of that summer I planned several weekends with the kids up at the Pocono house, with mixed results.

Mom and I were getting along during this time because she now had another target to focus on. Chris would make each scheduled visitation as difficult as possible, to a point where I dreaded making that phone call to outline my plans with the kids. Mom suggested that we take Dawn and Denise up to the house for the weekend and their mother Betty would join us. I felt a little uncomfortable, but I thought it would be good for the girls to see that Betty and I could work together for their benefit. The past few months had been tough on everybody, and my schedule left little time for them. We actually had a good time. The girls were able to coax their mom into the canoe, and Betty always knew how to make the girls laugh.

Dealing with Chris on visitation issues was always exhausting. I could never extract a simple yes from her. If I wanted to pick up the kids at nine in the morning, it was inconvenient for unknown reasons. If I wanted to bring them back at eight in the evening, she would have a problem with that. I remember one weekend when I wanted to take Ed up to the Pocono house so he could accompany me on a spring turkey hunt. I knew better than to mention anything about guns, and defined it as a "guys" weekend in the woods. She was immediately unhappy about my not including Nicolle. I offered to make a future date with Nicolle, but that wasn't to her liking either. I found myself wondering why I even tried to talk to her, and ultimately let my attorney handle the constant problems. Which he was happy to do. And happy to bill me for.

Ed Jr. and I ultimately had a great time. I woke him up at four thirty on Saturday morning, dressed him in some camouflage clothes I'd bought for him, had breakfast and went into the woods before sunrise. We sat quietly until the sun came up, when I started calling the birds. The sound of me "clucking" made him smile, but we never saw any turkeys. My calling did arouse the interest of a black bear and her cub, which worried me and literally scared the crap out of Ed Jr. I loaded him back into the truck and headed back to the house so he could get a change of clothes and a fast shower.

That night we went to a local restaurant for dinner, and on Sunday afternoon we headed back for Long Island. As I drove up to the house I saw a man coming out the front door. He turned to kiss Chris on the cheek and quickly got into his car and left. I didn't make an issue out of it at that time, but reserved the right to do so at a later date. I unloaded the car and was about to bring Ed Jr. up the front steps when he suddenly burst into tears. I asked him why he was crying and he told me that he didn't want the weekend to end. "Me too, son, but you have school tomorrow," I told him. On my way back to my apartment, I made a promise to schedule more of these special weekends with the kids.

Several days later I picked Ed Jr. up for soccer practice. We made small talk about our weekend together, and I asked him what his mother and sister did on the weekend while we were away. He told me they spent some time with mom's new friend. I let the subject drop. I didn't really care what Chris did with her life, as long as it didn't impact the welfare of my children. I had started to date, but I didn't want to confuse the kids by bringing another woman into the picture so soon after their mother and I had separated. That would change in the not too distant future.

When soccer practice ended that day, I was approached by Michael's mother, Barbara. She wanted to speak with me and asked her son and Ed Jr. to kick the ball around for a few minutes while we adults talked. She thanked me for the special attention I had given her son, and went on to define what she saw in me. "You are in my eyes the definition of the perfect father and husband." I muttered that there were several women who would dispute that statement, and we both laughed. I was getting a little uncomfortable and asked that she get to the point. She simply wanted to introduce me to a friend, who'd been divorced for many years and had a nine year old daughter. She's Italian, she added. I told her I had already discredited myself with two nationalities and wasn't ready or willing to begin the process again. She laughed and asked me to think about it.

I saw Barbara at practice each succeeding week, and she never failed to ask me if I was ready to call her friend. I always said no. On the day of the last soccer game in early June, she came over with a gift from the kids, which was customary. I knew I wouldn't see her again until the new season started. As she turned to walk away, she said, "Last chance. Sure you don't want to give my friend Janice a call?"

"I give up," I said. "Give me her number and I'll think about it."

"No more thinking, just call her," she shot back.

"Does she nag, like you do?"

"Probably!"

I tucked the piece of paper in my pocket and didn't find it until several days later when I did my laundry. I was learning to make sure that my pockets were empty before washing my jeans. Forgetting had meant pink underwear several weeks before. I put the phone number aside and didn't pick it up again until days later. The week had flown by and it was a Sunday evening.

I dialed the number and she picked up on the first ring. I introduced myself and told her that Barbara had insisted that I call her. She indicated that Barbara exercised the same pressure on her. I tried to make light of it, and suggested that the only way we would rid ourselves of Barbara would be to actually go out on a date. She didn't laugh, and indicated her willingness to get together the following week, on Tuesday around seven. I marked the calendar and noticed the date: June 14, my dad's birthday. An omen, I wondered? If so, is it a good one or a bad one?

I drove up to the two-story house on Oakfield Avenue in North Bellmore at seven sharp, and rang the upstairs bell. I was invited up and Janice introduced me to the babysitter, and then introduced me to her 10-year-old daughter, Deana. She was sitting on the couch, working on a needlepoint project, staring at a partially completed jigsaw puzzle and watching TV at the same time. Multi-tasking at such a young age! I was impressed.

Janice's parents lived several blocks away. She told the sitter to call them if she needed anything. We drove out to Farmingdale to a restaurant called the 56th Fighter Group. It was located on the Republic Airport compound and was filled with World War II photos and memorabilia. Conversation during the drive out there was light, and now it was forced at best.

After two drinks and two hours I suggested we stop for coffee on the way back to her house. We sat in a booth in the back and drank coffee for several more hours. She talked about her daughter, her family, her friends and her job. She mentioned the Monday night card game with her girlfriends that went back over 10 years. I got the impression that she was happy with her life as it was, and didn't want to change it in any way. Confident, yet defensive. Sensing that the first date jitters were starting to subside, I suggested a dinner date for the following Saturday. She said, "Fine", and I drove back to her place, walked her to the door and said goodnight. On the way back to my apartment I decided that this was just another date, and while I would still take her to dinner come Saturday, I would not see her again after that.

The week went by quickly, and it was Saturday afternoon. A friend had dropped by to check in on me. As we were talking, the phone rang. It was Janice. She was ill, a virus or something and had to cancel our date. I told her to feel better and said I would call in a few days to reschedule. Later that afternoon, I went out to dinner by myself. I was getting pretty good at that. I was back home by eight and decided to call to see how she was feeling. It wasn't a good idea to make that call. She apparently thought that I was calling to see if she was really at home sick.

"Did you think I got a better offer," she asked?

"No, I just went out for a quick bite and came back home."

"Right. A single guy staying home on a Saturday night."

"Uh, yeah if I have nothing to do. Calling you was a bad idea. I meant well. Feel better. Bye for now."

I looked at the phone in disbelief. Are all women nuts these days? Just what I needed—an attitude just because I called to see if she was feeling better. By Monday night I had convinced myself that she was probably irritable because she was sick, and I'd follow up with a "How are you?" phone call and reschedule our dinner date. Bad idea again! I'd forgotten that Monday night was card night, and while she answered the phone, she quickly reminded me that she had told me about her weekly card games.

"Can't talk now," she said. Click.

I'm done with this woman, I thought. I've had enough abuse in my life. Don't need it. Don't want it and fuck it!

Mom and me. Niagara Falls, 1949

CHAPTER

16

I needed to clear my head of divorce and work issues, so I packed the car on a Thursday afternoon and drove up to the Pocono house for the long Fourth of July weekend. The previous week had been filled with meetings with my attorney discussing the rough outline of a separation agreement that would ultimately be incorporated into a divorce decree.

I found the demands from her attorney to be onerous, and the restrictions placed on my visitation to be ridiculous. I was beginning to understand why some dads just gave up and skipped town. One of the restrictions required that I maintain my primary residence within 50 miles of the children's residence, and I was required to get prior permission before I took the kids more than 50 miles from their home during visitation. It would be tantamount to kidnapping them.

The Pocono house was 118 miles from their home, so I understood her motivation from the outset. She also wanted to make sure I didn't move to Pennsylvania to avoid my obligations to her and the kids.

I arrived at the Pocono house around 7 p.m. and unpacked the car. I placed all my provisions for the

weekend by the side door and went down to the base-
ment to turn on the electricity. I hit the main breaker
and no lights. No power also meant no water and no
refrigerator. My neighbor Mark came to the door to
let me know that lightning had struck the power pole
between our houses. At his place, every light bulb had
exploded, his refrigerator was fried and the well water
pump burned out. The damage from this one act of
nature would cost him about $10,000 to repair.

I stared at him and said nothing, but I was thinking
about my own financial situation. Even if my insurance
covered part of the damage, I was living from month to
month in those days, and had little money to fall back
on. At that moment the power came back on, and we
were amazed to find my house unscathed by the lightning. Everything worked right down to the last light
bulb. Was my luck about to change for the better? I
hoped so. I invited him and his family to use my facilities over the weekend and poured my first scotch.

The next morning I played nine holes at Pocono
Manor with another neighbor. We were done by 11
a.m. and the total cost with a motorized golf cart was
$11. Everything was less expensive up there, but so
were the salaries. No, I thought, I'll continue to work
and live on Long Island for the foreseeable future.

On Saturday afternoon I was expecting a friend to
arrive for the remainder of the weekend. She worked at
one of the many pubs in Westbury and we had become
friends. My divorce had been messy, stretching over a
painful five years. She had experienced the exact oppo-
site with her ex-husband. He just disappeared one day,

rather than sticking around and living up to his legal and moral obligations.

We had great respect for each other, and our conversations had therapeutic value. The rest of the weekend was spent walking in the woods, sunning in the canoe, and consuming lots of alcohol and good food. On Monday morning, we climbed into our respective cars feeling relaxed, refreshed and renewed. Back to Long Island and back to the bullshit.

Tuesday morning I came into the office ready to take on the world. I was on a high from the weekend and didn't want it to go away. My life had been filled with lows for years, and the highs were few and far apart, so I wanted them to last. This was one of the good days: My secretary would be transferring to another area of the bank that day, I hadn't been threatened by Chris and her attorney in almost a week, the Pocono house survived the lightning and I was due for my annual salary review later in the day.

I worked through the morning, broke for lunch with my boss, and came back to the office on an extended high partially induced by alcohol. My review was completed over two drinks and lunch, my salary increase was more than I expected, and the boss gave me credit for a great job under extenuating circumstances. "God, you can take me now," I thought. "It can't get much better than this." I was wrong again.

I arrived back at the office around 2 p.m. and returned a few phone calls. I met with a prospective client for about an hour and poured a cup of coffee as I watched him drive out of the parking lot. My secretary came into the office and told me she had a Mrs. Kirchner on hold.

"Kirchner?" I didn't recognize the name.

"She says she knows you and wanted to speak with you for a minute."

Debbie looked down at the piece of paper in her hand and read the name again. Janice Kirchner. She had the last name wrong, but now I knew who it was. I just didn't know what it was about. I looked at the blinking light on the phone and wondered just how long I should wait before picking up the call. Maybe she would get tired of waiting and hang up. Of course, if that happened, I'd never know why she decided to call me. Where did she get my office number anyway? No matter, I figured, and picked up the receiver.

"This is Ed Mirabella," I said in my most professional and indifferent voice.

"Hi, Ed, this is Janice. Do you have time to talk?"

I had a few minutes, I replied, and asked why she had called.

"I want to apologize for the way I spoke to you," she said, "and wondered if we could get together again and start all over."

Before I could think about what she said, the word "sure" came out of my mouth.

"How about tomorrow? OK, what time? I'll pick you up around 6:30," I said, thinking we would go to dinner, but not saying it. She said she would be ready, and said goodbye. "Dammit, Ed, why did you sound so eager," I thought, kicking myself mentally.

I guess I was caught off guard when she apologized for her less than flattering attitude when we had spoken three weeks earlier. I also was totally unfamiliar with exactly how to deal with a woman who could admit that she was wrong. It never happened to me before. What's her motive? She surely wants little to do with a man who has two failed marriages and four children. What's the expression? Too much baggage. Well, I'll find out tomorrow, I thought, and went back to work.

At 5 p.m., Deb poked her head into my office to say goodnight and goodbye. I wished her well in her new job, and she thanked me and added, "By the way, did you ever figure out where you met Mrs. Kirchner? "Yes I did," I said, without offering an explanation. She didn't ask for one, either.

The following day I was in a conference until 6 p.m. and barely made it to Janice's house on time. I honked the horn this time, which is as rude now as it was then. I guess I had something to prove, but I still couldn't figure out what. She came down and as she walked to the car I reached over from the driver's seat and pushed the passenger door open.

As she stepped into the car I looked over and said, "I've got something to say to you before you close that door. I've been around the block a few times and have the scars to prove it. I'm not into playing games, so if you're OK with that, we can try to get to know each other and maybe, just maybe, enjoy each other's company."

She closed the door, put on her seat belt and asked where were going? "To dinner," I said. "I've already had dinner," she replied. "I haven't," I said and pulled away from the curb.

I drove to a local Chinese restaurant where I ate like a "caffone" while she sipped on a drink. We talked that night until the early hours of the morning. I brought her home, said goodnight at the door and waited until the upstairs light went on. On the way back home I thought to myself, "We'll see, we'll see."

The next day I couldn't stop thinking about her and the great conversation we'd had the night before. I wanted to call her but I didn't. Later in the week I did call and set a date for that weekend. Over dinner we talked about her family, her daughter Deana, and then, finally, why her marriage had failed. Deana was only 2 when she asked her husband to leave. She'd decided one day that she had simply had enough of the uncertainty and disappointment, and knew that her family would always be there for her and her daughter. Without having met them, I knew they had to be special people, and would find out soon enough that the word "special" was a gross understatement.

Soon we found ourselves talking on a daily basis, disappointed if we missed a day. I remember dropping her off on a Saturday night and telling her that I would talk to her during the week. One Monday night she called and asked me what I was doing. I told her I had laundry to do. She immediately asked me to bring it to her, and we could have coffee while the washing machine did the rest.

"You never know what people wash in those Laundromat machines," she said.

So true: I remember itching for days after my mother washed fiberglass curtains once. The residue in the machine made for an uncomfortable few days until she figured out what had happened.

I packed my dirty clothes into my bachelor-sized basket, threw my little bottles of detergent, fabric softener and bleach on top and drove to her house. Jan and Deana both laughed when they saw me walking up to the door with my tiny basket that contained maybe 10 articles of clothing.

She took the basket from me and told me to go upstairs with Deana. Two minutes later she was back and the coffee was delicious. We sat at her kitchen table and talked like we hadn't spoken in months. There was always something positive in her tone. This lady always saw the glass of life half full, not half empty.

Several days later, she called and invited me for a Sunday dinner with her and Deana. "Nothing special, just pasta, meat balls and Italian bread," she said. It sounded great to me. "I'll bring the wine," I offered.

I was a pretty accomplished cook myself, but it wasn't much fun cooking for one, so I usually just prepared the basics or ordered Chinese food on occasion. When I was little, I remember helping mom and dad prepare the holiday meals. Dad worked at the old Grotto Azurra on Mulberry Street in the early 1940s, and I was amazed at how good he was with a knife and the various Italian recipes he had experience with, especially the fish that dominated Christmas Eve in those days. I learned a lot from him about cooking and never forgot. I also remember those times as happy occasions, when mom was full of the holidays and less full of herself. She showed approval of what dad was able to do in the kitchen, and I wished back then that every day was Christmas. They both looked happy on those special days.

On Sunday morning the phone rang, and it was Jan. She'd called to ask if I ate my meat with the pasta or after, as a second dish. She also wanted to know if I ate my salad as an appetizer or with my meal. I had never really thought about that before. I replied that it didn't really matter, but she wouldn't accept my reply. "OK, I have my pasta first, and then have the salad with the meat." Fine she said, I'll see you about two. As I got off the phone I found myself thinking about the meal sequence at my house. Yes, we did it the same way, as did the rest of my family.

That first home-cooked meal with Jan and Deana gave me the opportunity to see how mother and daughter related to each other. They were especially close, as you would expect with an only child and a single parent. I thought of my own history as an only child, but there were no similarities in our relationships. How sad. Deana was a bit shy, but I was able to get her involved in a conversation when I mentioned that I had four kids, and went on to tell her a little about each of them. In age, Deana fit right in the middle, a fact that made her smile. I also told her she would get to meet them at some point. She immediately asked, When? Jan came to the rescue with a "we'll see," followed by a quick change in the subject: "So, Ed, tell me about your Pocono house."

The rest of that first summer was filled with work and visits with my kids, and I spent any free time I had with Jan. One night she asked me to pick her up at her parents' house, which was only two blocks away from where she lived. Jan and Deana were staying there—house sitting, feeding the dog—while her parents were up at Saratoga.

When I arrived, I walked up the driveway toward the back of the house. Jan and Deana were on the rear deck with Jan's maternal grandmother. Grandma Sadie looked me straight in the eye and said, "Not too late, she's got to work tomorrow." The look on her face and the tone in her voice sent a clear message. I immediately asked her what time she expected Jan home. "Use your judgment," she said. The next day Jan advised me of her grandmother's approval, especially my clean and shined shoes, which apparently meant something to an Italian octogenarian. I was going to tell her I also changed my underwear daily, but thought better of it.

Labor Day weekend came way too fast that year, but at least I was invited to Jan's parents' house for a barbecue. Who will be there, I asked? She rattled off the names of relatives and friends for a few minutes. I asked if Grandma Sadie would be there. Of course, she said, asking why I wanted to know. My reply made her laugh: "I'll remember to shine my shoes!"

I arrived on time with both arms filled with several bottles of wine and two boxes of cake. It reminded me of an old Italian saying: When you visit special people for dinner, make sure you have to ring the doorbell with your elbow. And I did. I was welcomed by Jan's mother, who introduced me to the family and friends. Jan's dad was hovering over the barbecue. He pointed to a cooler and told me to grab a beer. I did and walked over to him to shake his hand. He handed me a cooked turkey breast on a platter, and asked if I knew how to carve. I said yes and spent the next 10 minutes slicing the turkey breast and feeding bits of it to the family dog, Sandy, who sat at my feet growling. He looked to be part pit bull, so I wasn't taking chances. Sandy and I got along well from that day on. The same applies to Marge and Joe Bongiorno, Jan's parents.

Hey, Grandma Sadie liked me, the dog liked me and, for the first time in a long while, I liked me.

Later that fall, we headed to the Pocono house for the weekend. During the winter of 1984, we loaded the kids in the Blazer for a weekend of ice skating on the frozen pond, plus some serious sledding. That trip almost ended our relationship. Two of the three kids got sick, and Jan was seriously evaluating if she could deal with what she would have to deal with if our relationship went to the next level. When she called to tell me, I simply said, "I understand." What else could I say? She was right, and she was thinking of all we would have to deal with. Ultimately we got through that time, and moved on, together.

When I arrived at the office on the Monday after Jan and I had taken the kids up to the house for some winter fun, I was a little preoccupied with the possibility that our relationship might come to an end. I couldn't blame her, but I had developed strong feelings and didn't want to lose her. As I mulled it over, my attorney called. He had received a call from Chris' lawyer regarding my weekend with the kids and my female companion. I simply told him that I didn't think it would be a problem: Chris had been seeing someone, too, and I had time-date stamped photos of him entering the house and leaving the following day. My attorney chuckled as I told him the best defense was and always had been a good offense. The subject was never brought up again.

Several days later, my lawyer was advised that Chris had fired her attorney and the new guy had already reached out to him. He was scrapping the separation agreement we had signed months before, and wanted to renegotiate several areas, all with dire consequences for me. We met several days later and walked out of the meeting within the first half hour. Ultimately a judge would decide our fate. At this point I just wanted it to be over, so I could get on with my life and spare the kids any additional emotional trauma. She was indeed living up to her promise to make my life miserable for as long as possible.

Finally, in November 1984, the divorce became final. Jan and I were still together. Our kids had gotten to know each other and really liked being together. I was spending more time with Jan during the week and a lot less time at the apartment. North Bellmore was only a few miles from my office in Garden City, so the overnight visits offered some additional fringe benefits. Being able to sleep a little later in the mornings felt great, as did the 10-minute drive instead my usual 45-minutes in heavy traffic. Her mom and dad had noticed my stays, but never said a word. Their daughter was happy and their granddaughter seemed happy also. The visits with her biological father were infrequent at best, and child support had been non-existent. He just didn't believe in it, and was getting away with it at that point. What balls!

CHAPTER

17

Mom had settled into a routine living in the Bensonhurst section of Brooklyn. Jan and I visited from time to time and they seemed to get along. My biggest fear involved mom's uncanny ability to piss people off. If she had the slightest idea that our relationship was serious, she would do anything to end it. On one of those visits I went into the living room to catch the end of a football game, while they chatted in the kitchen. Big mistake! Mom had Jan all to herself and stated very clearly that she never wanted to see me get married again.

"After all," she said, "he has four children and immense financial responsibilities, and shouldn't ever take on any more."

Two minutes later when I came back into the kitchen Mom announced that she had met someone through the Deaf Blind Association and was thinking about getting married. It didn't hit me right away because I was trying to visualize a room full of people afflicted with those handicaps. The dance floor at their socials had to be a hoot. I should call Benny Hill and tell him to get his camera ready. Mom promised to bring Joe out to visit us the following week.

The ride back to Bellmore was extremely quiet. Jan had little to say, and I urged her to tell me what was bothering her. She related the conversation to me and I apologized for my mother's senseless words. I promised myself that I would make sure that it didn't happen again. Mom brought her friend Joe the following week, and we found him to be a remarkable person. He was born deaf, used sign language and had developed the ability to speak a bit. He was 10 years mom's junior, although I doubt he ever knew because she didn't look her age—she was better at causing premature aging in others.

They were married in May of 1984 and soon after purchased a one-bedroom condo in a new development in New Jersey. She had her new husband to focus on and they now lived 75 miles away. Just maybe she would lighten up on me.

But I didn't hold my breath.

The summer went by quickly, and I tried to spend more time with the kids. The court hearings always wore me out and left me depressed for days after. These were the times when I wanted to be alone. When I was working, I could put it all aside, but at the end of the day all the problems and issues would re-emerge. Just seeing the kids would be a reminder of an unpleasant past. For their sake, I had to make sure that history wouldn't repeat itself again. They never asked to be born and most certainly didn't deserve a life filled with uncertainty when it came to their father. Betty and I were always able to discuss issues without cursing, threats or innuendo. We could also agree to disagree. I don't remember a time when either of us tried to convince the girls to take sides.

With Chris it was very different. Threats were a part of my daily life after we separated. Ed and Nicolle were told terrible things about their dad. I started to dread the words, "Mommy said." They had been told that their father didn't care about them, didn't love them, because if he did he wouldn't have left us for that other woman and her child. They were told that Dad cared more for this other woman and her daughter than he does for you.

I had left Chris because I could no longer live with Chris. It had nothing to do with anyone else at the time. I used to tell the kids, "Your mom is a good woman and I'm not a bad man." I avoided fighting fire with fire. After our divorce became final in November 1984, I tried to settle into a regimen with the kids, but their mother never stopped the constant threats, and ultimately I surrendered to a life where I saw the kids infrequently. I knew in my heart that at some point in time they would understand. I hoped they wouldn't hate me for the life they had to endure. All children that are products of divorce are traumatized in some way. If the breakup is hostile—and most are—the scars they carry could impact them forever.

Ed Jr. was the constant topic of conversation regarding school, where he had problems. His grades were poor and his behavior was always a topic of discussion. Nicolle, on the other hand, seemed to do little to cause concern. I assumed that all was well, but the signs of her feeling abandoned were there. Very often on visits she would curl up on the couch and fall asleep. She was extremely quiet, and when asked about it she would always say that she was tired. Ed Jr. was the "squeaky wheel," and therefore received most of the grease. To a child's eyes it appeared Ed Jr. was more important, and Nicolle felt ignored and left out. That was never true, but it was how she felt. The effects would become obvious later and would have to be dealt with.

Dawn headed off to college in 1984. Two years earlier, when she was a junior in high school, I happened to be serving on a corporate development committee at Hofstra University and was able to get her into the school's Ambassador Program, which was designed to give a student a chance to spend several days on campus. They would be teamed up with an upper classman and follow the daily routine, attending classes, meals and sleeping in the dorm overnight. Dawn loved the experience, as did her boyfriend at the time. They were both accepted, and graduated together four years later. As the oldest, Dawn always provided positive motivation to her sisters and brother. Keeping the family together, though not easy to do, was always a priority for her.

Denise was as different from Dawn as night is to day. She was bold, argumentative and determined to do what she wanted as far back as I can remember. Her premature birth and early health problems probably caused us to handle her gently, rather than take a tougher stance. I was out of the picture soon after her birth, and her mom did what she could in raising our daughters. There are no rule books for parents, and we very often reacted, rather than acted. When I was called into a conference with her and her mom, it was usually too late to do much. I would lecture, cajole and scold, but received only a blank stare in return. Her stare told me that she had no problem defying me. I would leave and head back to Long Island and Denise would go right back to doing what she wanted. She left high school at 16, only to go back and finish years later. She found her way and in her own time.

With Ed Jr. and Nicolle the constant battle with their mother made it impossible to be effective as a non-custodial parent, so in 1985 I launched a custody battle that achieved absolutely nothing. Fathers don't get much in the way of sympathy in the court system, and the reasons for my custody suit were dismissed in short order. The 50-mile restriction placed on me remained. After a Sunday visit with their grandmother in New Jersey, I received a call from my attorney because I had violated the 50 mile rule. Chris had called her attorney and the police. "Jesus Christ, I took them to see their grandmother," I explained.

In 1991, Chris decided to start a new life in Indianapolis. She sold the house and moved and there was nothing I could do about it. The rules were different for mothers, at least according to the court system. I was reminded that I must however continue to live up to my financial obligations, no matter where they lived. I was devastated, and finally realized that she was still doing her best to make my life miserable, but at the cost of two children. My visits were over unless I wanted to fund airline tickets so they could visit me from time to time. As a result, I did not see Ed Jr. and Nicolle for the next 18 months. Dawn was married to Joe in 1991, and wanted her brother and sister at the wedding. I just couldn't afford it at the time, and knew from past experience just how difficult it would be to get it done. Chris always wanted something in return before she would grant me visitation.

Eighteen months later, Chris and the kids were back on Long Island. The move to Indianapolis had been a disaster. No one would hire a New Yorker when there was massive unemployment in Indiana. The kids struggled in school, where everything was different. Chris ate through a big chunk of the money from the sale of the house, and somehow concluded that the whole thing was my fault. Surprise, surprise! She petitioned for more child support as soon as the alimony term had expired, and got a sizeable increase. I didn't mind paying for my mistakes, but now I was expected to pay for hers as well.

I often thought of packing up and moving to another state, but that was what other dads did, including Jan's ex-husband. He ran to Florida where he lived unscathed for the next 25 years rather than pay child support. He did pay a heavy price for his decision. He never got to see a beautiful child grow into a wonderful woman. I had that honor, because Jan and I were married in 1985. I would finally have an opportunity to be a full time father to one of five children. In 1993, I legally adopted 19-year-old Deana while she was attending Oneonta State University. The adoption was finalized in the same court buildings in Mineola that I had visited so many times since 1983.

This time I walked down the courthouse steps with my wife and new daughter with a big smile on my face.

First Communion, 1950, with Mom, Dad,
Aunt Mary, and Uncle Tom

CHAPTER

18

After mom married Joe, they planned a vacation trip to Tennessee for February 1985 to visit some relatives that had not met Mom. Jan's parents were on vacation in Florida at the same time. I was sitting in the living room watching TV and looking over the divorce decree that had finally arrived in the mail. We had discussed marriage several times, but never really set a date. The past year had been bearable because of the support that Jan provided. I knew that we loved each other, but setting a date and making plans would result in all sorts of bullshit that neither of us wanted to endure.

I looked over at her and simply said, "Let's get married."

"OK, but when?" Jan replied.

"Next week," I said quickly.

"But our parents are away," she protested.

"Exactly," I said.

Within three days, we had our blood tests and a marriage license. We found a justice of the peace, asked Jan's brother John and his wife to be our witnesses, and were married in her living room on Saturday Feb. 9. Our reception consisted of dinner at our favorite

Chinese restaurant in Levittown followed by a phone call to Jan's parents in Florida to give them the news. Their reaction was one of approval, and my father-in-law planned a celebratory dinner for the immediate family after they returned from Florida.

I would wait for Mom and Joe to return from Tennessee to tell them. I was afraid of Mom's reaction, and wanted to spare my wife the unsettling remarks that most certainly would be made. Later that night we drove to a friend's house to tell them. It was Jan's closest friend, Cathy—who had convinced her to call me and apologize after our first dinner date had been cancelled and the abrupt phone call several days later. Cathy was ecstatic for us, and we toasted the future together with a glass of Champagne. They took a picture to commemorate the date, and it still hangs in our home.

For Italians, we had broken just about every tradition. But we knew from experience that big weddings with gowns and tuxedos, flowers and hundreds of guests do not ensure a long, happy life together. We were both tired of doing what was expected and right, and decided to try it our way. Our honeymoon consisted of two days at the Pocono house during an ice storm that literally had us trapped inside the cabin.

Not such a bad thing when you want to be alone together.

Dawn and Denise received the news with smiles, hugs and kisses. Ed Jr. and Nicolle didn't really know how to react. Only time would show them what Jan was made of, and that would have to be good enough under the circumstances. Mom took the news with a jaundiced eye, and made the fatal mistake of saying "Well, if you want my opinion …" I stopped her in mid sentence. "No, Mom," I said, "I don't want your opinion." I had to control her as best I could right from the outset. Any attempt to drive a wedge between Jan and I would result in her losing me as a son. My loyalty could not be questioned. My wife came first, then the kids. It stopped there. She would behave for once.

We settled into a small Cape Cod in Wantagh, and within 18 months had sold the Pocono house. The trips up there had become exhausting and the kids were getting older and had other things on their minds. I got along real well with my in-laws and spent quite a bit of time with them. My father-in-law would join me on hunting trips and was always available to help me with home improvements. Considering him a trusted adviser, I asked his advice on my pending custody suit. I remember his words of caution to this day. "Ed, don't open up a can of worms." I didn't listen to him, but he never said "I told you so."

On Sundays we were often together for dinner. Pop and I would bet the ponies at the local OTB, come home for dinner and watch the remaining races on TV. I had a closer relationship with him than I did with my own father, because no one was interfering. Jan and I loved his drop-by visits for coffee with us on Saturdays or Sundays. But just when things looked good, a string of events terminated those good times.

My step dad was a bull of a man who would take on any job that required brute force. I can remember the partially submerged log in the pond at the Pocono house. The canoe would get stuck on it every time we tried to push off from the bank or come back in. Papa Joe, as he was called, waded out into the water grabbed onto what turned out to be a tree trunk and started dragging it out of the way. As he pulled it up onto the bank he laughed at his own strength—the tree was over 12 feet long and at least a foot in diameter. His body was covered with black mud. He laughed again and took the garden hose to wash himself off. Our water supply came directly from an artesian well, and was always ice cold. Nothing fazed that man, and that's why we weren't the least bit concerned when he went into the hospital for a minor surgical procedure in the summer of 1991. I can still remember my shock when the voice on the other end of the phone advised me that he had suffered a massive heart attack. He was gone in 18 hours, and mom would be widowed again. She wailed at the hospital, at the funeral home and at the cemetery. Her grief was real, and she mourned this loss for a long time. She never mourned my father's death with this kind of intensity.

Dawn and Joe were married later that year, and Mom was understandably saddened that Joe never got to see her walk down the aisle. I tried to support her through this tough time, but as usual it was never enough in her eyes. I made the 150-mile round trip to Jersey on a weekly basis in the beginning. "There's so much to do and I need your help, Edward," Mom said. Trips to the stores, doctors, the cemetery, a never ending list. She was completely oblivious to my own responsibilities. I used to tell clients of mine at the bank to avoid over-diversifying their businesses, because you spread your resources too thinly. That's exactly what was happening to me again.

During the next six years, Jan and I lost most of our senior generation of relatives. It started in 1993 when Grandma Sadie passed, followed by my father-in-law in 1996. Between 1996 and 2003, when Jan's mother passed, we lost most of our aunts and uncles on both sides of the family, in addition to a cousin who was only in his 40s. Our own sense of mortality was awakened and that was a sobering experience. My mom was the oldest among the living, and she was also losing her closest friends at an alarming pace. We had lived most of our adult lives without experiencing the loss of loved ones, and now they were all gone. I had turned 60, and found each day at work to be exhausting. I needed to work another three years before I could consider retirement. If all of the aforementioned wasn't enough, I was now facing criticism from some of my own children, who now had children of their own. They were too quick to point out that my mother, their Nani was my responsibility, and I wasn't doing enough to help her. Mom had voiced her dissatisfaction with me to anyone who would listen. She would also complain about her grandchildren who never visited, although she had been "helpful and generous" with all of them. There was only one person who never faced criticism and was perfect in Moms' eyes, and that was and is my oldest daughter.

Dawns' devotion to her grandmother defies logic and reasoning, and makes her a special person. She sees past her grandmother's faults and cherishes every moment that she shares with her. When her patience is tested, she gets past it very quickly. That's the way it has always been between the two of them, and that's the way it will always be.

Then, there's the rest of us. No matter how hard the other kids tried, they were always unfavorably compared to Dawn. Ultimately, one of them just gave up. Denise felt like a second class citizen when she was a child, and as an adult would see her grandmother only when necessary. Ed Jr. and Nicolle, by virtue of circumstance, never formed a bond with their grandmother. Their mother made that impossible.

Then there is Deana, who came into the family at 10 years of age. I guess Mom put her in a special category. She didn't visit any more than the others, but also never suffered my mother's criticism. I defended all the kids when Mom got on the subject, because I saw the bigger picture and because I had lived with her dissatisfaction all my life. Dawn had to accept the fact that we don't see things as she does. We are all different for various reasons, and shouldn't be condemned for what we don't do.

When I think about it now, I'm amazed that Mom never realized that it was all her doing, but she would never admit to having made mistakes. Here she would prove me wrong.

CHAPTER

19

On April 30, 2006, I walked out of my office at the First National Bank of Long Island, ending a career in banking that spanned 43 years. I always said that I would choose my own time for retirement and had made the decision back in December. The industry had changed and I no longer liked going to work each day, although I gave it my best right until I surrendered the keys to the company car. Now Jan was parked outside to take me home. As I walked toward the car, I saw that beautiful smile that I fell in love with 21 years earlier. As we drove south on Route 106, I took in the sight of the beautiful homes, golf courses and horse farms that define Brookville. I had driven that route constantly during the previous nine years, but that day I appreciated the beauty in a different way. I was retired. Deep down inside I knew I was lying.

Several months before I notified the bank of my retirement date, I had been working on a project at the County Clerk' office in Mineola. The sign next to the door asked that visitors turn off all cell phones before entering. I complied and started to work on the research project that brought me to that building. After two hours I had this nagging feeling that someone was trying to reach me, so I took a break and turned on the phone as I left the building. It rang immediately. It was my oldest daughter Dawn. All she said was, "Dad I have cancer." It may have been a few seconds, but it felt like an hour before I could speak. I tried my best to stay calm, to offer some comforting words, but I knew internal melanoma was very often fatal. She would consult at Sloan Kettering the following week. I told her I would call her when I got home.

I climbed into the car and screamed until I was hoarse. I yelled at the heavens. "Test me all you want, but please leave my daughter alone. My children have dealt with enough in their lives." Finally drained, I drove home and fell into my wife's arms.

The next few months were tough for all of us. I made the decision not to tell Mom about Dawn's illness. She had just celebrated her 91st birthday, and was dealing with a new malady that would ultimately take her sight. Deaf and now going blind was enough for her to bear, I decided. She would constantly ask why Dawn hadn't visited in awhile, and I always came up with an acceptable excuse. Dawn had her surgery and started the long road to recovery. We watched and prayed. I wasn't much good at anything anymore, because I was preoccupied with my daughters' grave illness and spent a lot of time in church, just praying for her. I was also saddled with the fact that Mom couldn't live alone in her upper-level condo much longer. I had found a local woman who would take her shopping, to the doctors, and occasionally bring her out to our house for a visit, but Mom was home and alone most of the week. Too much time for something bad to happen, I figured. I'd lie awake at night picturing her at the bottom of the stairs after a fall, or slipping on the ice as she went to fetch the mail. Then my thoughts would turn to Dawn. I didn't sleep much during those days. I had to do something during the day to get my mind off the horror of possibly losing a child. I also needed to supplement my retirement income.

Truth is, we couldn't live well on Social Security and a small pension. We could just get by each month. I had contributed to my 401K for 20 years, but never at the level that others did. I blame no one for the path I took in life, and always knew that I would never be able to retire totally, nor did I want to. For now I would take a few months off, take a vacation and start my next career at the end of the summer. June and July were filled with all the "honey do" projects that needed to be attended to around the house. By the time August came around I was getting itchy and started to look for some other things to do that would also generate additional income.

The phone rang on a Wednesday morning in August. It was an old business associate who asked if I was interested in doing some consulting. Several days later we met for breakfast and hammered out the outline for a consulting arrangement. I had my first client, and something to keep me busy and earning one or two days a week. I still had time to visit my mother, get away with Jan on mini vacations and play a little golf. Soon I was up to four clients, and the workload started to eat into my free time. But I was only 63, and never wanted to vegetate at home like so many of my associates did after retirement. I needed to keep my mind and body active.

Dawn was recovering, and the results of her last three-month checkup showed no sign of the cancer. Every three months going forward we would wait for the results, and she would call us as soon as she heard from the doctors. A clean report would make us smile, but as she got closer to the next round of tests, our level of concern would be elevated again.

During the latter part of 2006 and into 2007, Mom lost 90 percent of her vision to macular degeneration. There were frequent trips to her ophthalmic surgeon and dozens of needles directly into the eyes to stop the progressive nature of the disease. Dawn took on handling most of the doctor visits. It took a load off my shoulders, and I always appreciated her help. Despite my constant appeal to the other kids, she received little help from them. Dawn was on heavy doses of Interferon, a form of chemotherapy that left her drained and tired for days after her treatments. I urged the other kids to help, but no amount of coaxing worked. The old scars were there. They had been denied the opportunity to bond with their grandmother or had seen her partiality towards the oldest and had given up trying to win equal status and acceptance.

As I saw my mother lose her sight, I also saw her loneliness deepen. She could no longer read a book or newspaper. The captioning on her TV was too small, so she ultimately gave up on that. Then there was the time she spent alone. Her visits to our house became rare, as I was in my mid-60s and starting to feel my own age. I was having trouble caring for her when she did visit, because I was now having trouble caring for myself. It started slowly for me with arthritis that left my hands stiff and painful. Next it was my eyes. Cataracts had diminished my vision to the point I was afraid to drive at night. Two surgeries later my vision was much improved, but severe back pain was diagnosed as spinal stenosis, and surgery was an option I refused. I lived on pain killers, muscle relaxers and steroids, with all the accompanying side effects.

Some of my children saw me as a parent who was shirking his responsibility towards his 91-year-old mother. They never saw me as a senior citizen with my own health issues, not to mention financial burdens that a 63-year-old didn't deserve. It was at this point during 2009 that I started to research an assisted living facility for Mom. I couldn't do it anymore, Dawn shouldn't have to do it without some help, and the rest of the kids didn't really seem to care. Who could object to a new safe environment with help and 24-7 care?

Dawn researched a long list of facilities while I started the massive Social Services process with the help of an Advocate for the Aged from the South Brunswick Senior Center.

Mom was against the move, and told everyone who would listen. Again, I was portrayed as the insensitive son. She received enough offers of help from family and friends that I ultimately terminated the process. Of course, none of the help materialized, and Mom was stuck in her little condo, which I paid to maintain, paid the taxes and insurance, and paid for part time homecare. I didn't mind the lack of recognition from her and others for what I did. I did, however, resent the criticism from people who didn't have the vaguest idea of what was going on.

After another year or so, it became clear Mom wasn't taking proper care of herself. She always put on makeup in the morning, fixed her hair and kept the condo neat, but her eating habits weren't good and her personal hygiene began to suffer because she was afraid she might fall in the bath tub. She was also making mistakes with her medications that might have proved fatal. Shopping trips to the supermarket were rare, so her freezer was well stocked, but leftovers that anyone else would discard were eaten well after the point at which they should have been thrown out. She was visibly slowing down and her memory was starting to wane. We would get phone calls from her constantly because the loneliness was maddening. She had a phone with large letters and numbers in her living room. She would dial, count to 15 and then start talking. The messages were always the same. "I need some human contact. No one visits me." We would answer through a special email receiver that would print our answers on sheets of paper in a font that was large enough for her to read. I knew it was time to broach the subject again.

Confirmation, 1954. Uncle Tom and Aunt Mary

CHAPTER

20

May 2010, and I was trying to visit Mom every two or three weeks.

During one of those visits I brought up the subject of assisted living again. She had insisted that I was trying to put her in a nursing home in the past, but this time she asked questions. I was patient and stressed that she wouldn't be alone for long periods of time. The daily activities ranged from exercise classes, to bingo and dance, and they even had a few slot machines on the third floor. That made her smile. We talked about her medication, too, because she was making more mistakes identifying her various pills. The nurses' station would remind her and dispense her pills on schedule. There was a doctor on staff if she became ill, and transportation to and from shopping, group lunches and Atlantic City. The food was restaurant quality, snacks available day and night, and the surrounding grounds had walking paths, gardens, a bocce court and vegetable gardens. She began to see that it was in no way a nursing home, but a residence with all the amenities included. I didn't want to exhaust her with more discussion, so I asked her to think on it for awhile and took her out to lunch.

We returned about an hour later. Burger King is her favorite fast food chain, and when you crave lunch at 11 in the morning you get in and out fast. She wanted to talk some more, so I listened as she recounted stories that took us back to the house on East 7th Street in Flatbush. She remembered when I had a newspaper route at age 11, and I reminded her that I had had another job at 10. She said, "That's right, you worked for tips at the Laundromat." She also remembered that I was saving those nickels and dimes for a folding knife to keep with my fishing tackle. I reminded her that it had a pearl handle and two different blades. Dad used to take me fishing off Steeplechase Pier in Coney Island. Her face changed suddenly, and I asked her if something was wrong. She looked at me, her eyes filling with tears.

"I broke the blade off that knife," she said, "and I'm so sorry. It was wrong. Do you remember that?" Yes Mom, I never forgot that day. I can still remember the look on your face when you snapped the blade. And now I could see the look on my face was still with her after 56 years. "I always knew it was wrong and I meant to apologize years ago, but I never focused on that event until just now," she said.

And then the flood gates opened with stories of all the people that thought she would be unable to care for a child because of her handicap. How her hearing loss left her feeling that she was imperfect or incomplete as a person. I was born in March of 1943. At that time my father was working the night shift at the Brooklyn Navy Yard. Ship building was in high gear after Pearl Harbor, and the money was good. Mom would tie a string to her wrist and attach the other end to my cradle before going to bed at night. Any movement of the cradle would awaken her to check on me. There were times that she was so starved for sleep that neighbors would come into the apartment to wake her when my movement didn't. My crying would disturb the other residents in the building. Eventually, Dad had to give up the shipbuilding job—it paid over $100 a week with overtime—and work at the local Rolstons Food Market for a mere $16 a week so that he could be home with her during the night. Because she felt flawed being deaf, I had to be perfect. I was her creation, and raising me would finally wash away the doubts that she had to deal with. Because she was deaf she had to have her eyes on me all the time. I began to realize that I made her whole. I was expected to communicate for her when her back was turned. She would have no way of knowing if someone was calling out to her. Through me, she could finally hear.

I looked at my watch and realized that we had been talking for an hour and a half. I also realized that her need for constant reinforcement from me and others would tell her that she had done a good job "for a deaf woman." Our conversation that day ended with an admission that she had been hard on me, and that I shouldn't have been saddled with so much responsibility from the time when I was old enough to talk. I was repeatedly told that I had to realize that my mother was deaf. After all these years Mom was figuring things out, and so was I. She had taken away a portion of my childhood, but that wasn't her intent. I told her that there isn't a rule book for parents. You do things because they feel right or make sense at the time. We also make mistakes. I kissed and hugged her, thanked her and climbed into the car for the long ride home.

I drove onto the turnpike heading north, but stayed in the right lane. The impact of what had just taken place hit me, and hit me hard. I saw the fright in her eyes. She had to know that this would be her last move, but she was ready for it. I also knew that I would miss her terribly when she passed, but we had settled some old issues that needed to be addressed. It came from her heart, and I let her know that I understood. There would be no regrets going forward. She understood her mistakes, and the reasons behind them. More important, I understood too.

I started the paperwork process with Social Services the next day. It would be the second time within two years, and a lot had changed. Her doctor had to certify her as needing Assisted Living services. "She's deaf and blind. Isn't that enough?" I asked. Funeral arrangements had to be made in advance. The look-back period for financial records was now five years, versus three years in the past. Finally, after three months of gathering and submitting information, Mom was approved for Medicaid, but only after all of her assets had been depleted. She had little left at this point in her life, so this requirement was easy to meet.

A week later, I took mom to the assisted living facility we had determined was the best for her needs. When I arrived at her apartment I noticed some boxes along the wall in the living room. She had started to pack up her personal belongings and had tagged several items with notes. These items were designated for particular people. For example, I had always admired a brass figurine of two deer that stood on her TV cabinet. The tag read "Ed." And so it went, item by item. There were other boxes that contained keepsakes and memories that she intended to take with her. Yes, she was ready to take the next step.

CHAPTER

21

Dawn's search for an appropriate assisted living facility had been an arduous one. If a facility emitted any foul odors, it was eliminated from the list. If the next place was more tuned to dementia patients, off the list. Finally, Dawn found a place that met all of her requirements, a facility that would guarantee that my mother could stay through the full end-of-life cycle. It was time to visit the facility with Mom.

It was early September 2011 when we drove into the parking lot of the facility in Shrewsbury. Mom squinted to take in the picturesque surroundings and we entered the lobby. She commented immediately that the design reminded her of a five-star hotel or a resort. After our tour we looked at her apartment, which she would share with another resident. They both had their own sleeping quarters, but shared the bath and kitchen. She was introduced to her roommate and they hit it off immediately. The only thing left was to schedule a move-in date, and that happened on Sept. 28, 2011.

Mom has thrived in her new environment since then, but still likes to complain about loneliness and infrequent visits from family members. Yes, she still likes to bitch, but then again, old habits are hard to break. Funny thing, she never complains about her new home. "They think I'm amazing, Edward," she told me.

She is, actually. We try to send her email messages that print onto white paper using a large font, helping keep her aware of things when we can't visit, and she will dial that phone with the very large numbers to tell us she received our message. Her short-term memory is starting to wane, because she will very often call us again five minutes later with the same message.

I sleep a lot better knowing that she is in a safe environment, staffed by people who care. Dawn has been cancer-free for over eight years now, and Mom never had to share the worry that consumed me and the rest of the family. Mom turned 97 in October and had one wish: A visit with her 101-year-old sister, Catherine. No, you can't make this stuff up. Truth is stranger than fiction—and more interesting too.

I'm still working part time, and find it enjoyable. I've developed another family of sorts through an economic development group that I joined over 35 years ago. About five years ago, I determined that it was time to bring in the third generation of young executives to ensure its future, and the ongoing development of new ideas in tough economic times. I call them, "my other family." They in turn seek my counsel on many issues, helping to make this senior citizen feel relavant and needed. They have taken the reins of our group during the past three years, and have taken it to new highs. I like sitting at the bar at events, and totally enjoy the fruits of their labor. My consulting clients are fewer these days, but those that are left have become friends. Working with and for them is rewarding and enjoyable.

Janice and I have a good marriage and a good life. We enjoy being together, but we also enjoy our own time. For me it's the gym, classic car shows and a little bit of the casinos. For her it's Zumba class with friends, our home, our grandchildren and, yes, the casinos, too. She continues to be my best friend, my strongest supporter and the oil on the water in turbulent times. Our relationship is built on trust, tons of love and a conscious decision to eliminate toxic people from our lives. We've had too much of that in the past, and there is too little time left.

Denise and her family live near Dawn in New Jersey. Ed Jr. is now living in northern Jersey, where he works as a stock broker. His last marriage failed in little over a year. When he isn't working, he spends lots of time with his best friend, his dog Dempsey, and stays in touch with the family. Nicolle is living with her fiancée here on Long Island and keeps busy making costume jewelry as a hobby and a minor source of income. Lastly, Deana and her family live a block away from Jan and I. As a result, we get to see her children quite often. Our other grandchildren live in New Jersey with their parents, so the visits are less frequent. Driving long distances is no longer the fun it used to be. It's now a chore that is put off as long as possible.

I celebrated my 70th birthday early this year, and I like to think of these pages as my special gift to my children. I'm hoping they will develop a greater level of understanding for their father at a much younger age than it took him to understand his own mother. Her love for me was undeniable, as is my love for my wife and children, and their children.

I'm sure my story isn't unique. I am sure, however, that it offers a different perspective of Dad's side of the story.

Prom Night 1960

Epilogue

Each generation forms a blueprint of what they would do differently at an early age. The formative years generate a deep impression of what we as individuals like and dislike. We are quick to condemn our parents for perceived injustices without a full understanding of what made them what they are. They also grew up dealing with parental issues that ultimately became an outline of how they would do things differently when it came time to raise their children, the next generation.

My father, Angelo Mirabella, was the sixth child born to Catarina Seresi Mirabella in 1908. She had five children from a prior marriage, and was left a widow in 1904. She met and married my grandfather, Carmelo Mirabella in 1906. He immigrated to the United States in 1909 when my father was 1, accompanied by my father's half brother, Michael Paci, who was 16 years old. They were to set up a home, start a business and at a later date bring my grandmother, four daughters and little Angelo to "Ameriga," where the streets were paved with gold and the trains ran in the sky. It was four years later before my father landed at Ellis Island, three days more before he stepped onto American soil.

Dad had little recollection of his father and was frightened at the sight of the large man with the handlebar mustache coming toward him with outstretched arms. He immediately ran into the arms of his mother and started to cry. My grandfather's reaction was one of anger. "The boy should know his own father. He is no son of mine," he said—words that stayed with my father all of his life. For the next 12 years he tried to win his father's approval, with little success. As a result he grew to become a quiet, withdrawn person. His half brother and sisters were all much older, and in 1924, after the death of his father, he dropped out of school. There was no one else at home to support his mother, so he took on that responsibility. With only an eighth-grade education, he could only work as a laborer on construction jobs or in a restaurant kitchen as a dish washer or waiter. He managed to hone his cooking skills and ultimately worked as a cook at La Grotta Azura on Mulberry Street in Manhattan. His meager salary of $16 a week was very often doubled because of tips he received from the Dorsey brothers—Tommy and Jimmy—whose band achieved major success in the 1930s and '40s. They enjoyed the Sicilian flair in Dad's cooking and would eat dinner at the restaurant several nights a week after their show. They always called Dad out of the kitchen to present him with a $5 tip after each meal.

Dad met my mother as a result of a friendship he cultivated with her brother, Tom. They were introduced to each other and dated on and off over several years. Dad was not an acceptable partner for Amelia "Mae"

Natoli in the eyes of my grandfather, who very often treated his daughters as personal chattel. Grandpa was apparently concerned that his daughter might take on the persona of the loose women that he cavorted with behind my grandmother's back. He saw her handicap as a weakness that men might prey on. What he didn't realize was the deep love my father had for my mother. They didn't see each other again for several years and Mom dated another man until his family decided a deaf girl was not suitable for their son. Mom was devastated by the breakup, and I often wondered if this was the "one true love" that she often spoke about.

Out for a walk one day, my father came face to face with my mother, and this time they didn't allow anything or anyone to come between them. They were married on Aug. 24, 1940. Early in 1941, Dad was drafted into the Army, but was classified as unsuitable for service because of a heart murmur. He later left the restaurant to work at Todd Shipyard, where many World War II naval vessels were built. I'll always remember him as a hard working man who was happiest when he was with his family, regardless of the fact that his wife, my mother, always ruled the roost.

Amelia Diana Natoli was born on Oct. 28, 1915, to Margaret and John Natoli. She was the third of four surviving children delivered by the local midwife. Three other children, twins and another boy, were stillborn, which was common in those days. Mom was known as Mae most of her adult life, although my grandfather called her "Black Head," for her jet-black hair, when he was angry. She was often in trouble because she would stand up to him, even defy him when she disagreed with the position he took on any issue. Many a loaf of Italian bread was tossed across the dinner table if he caught her mimicking his conversation, or imitating his constant grooming of his mustache.

She would entertain her sisters and brother with her antics, which amused her mother but were a further annoyance to Papa. Her defiance of his rules led to major embarrassment when she ran into her father on a subway train. She was in her late teens and was with some friends when he spied her wearing lipstick. His daughters were forbidden to wear makeup of any kind. He walked across the aisle, took his handkerchief out of his jacket pocket and proceeded to wipe the lipstick off, leaving her with a large red stain that covered most of her face. Before he returned to his seat on the other side of the subway car, he told her that he would deal with her more severely when she returned home. Mom did notice that he didn't mind the makeup on the woman that he was flirting with when she first boarded the train.

His rules were simple. "Do as I say, not as I do." By the time she returned home that day, my grandmother had quelled his anger, and nothing further was said. He did, however, glare at his daughter for several days afterward.

Mom also saw the different way her father related to his only son, Tom. While the three sisters adored their brother, he was in many ways cut from the same mold as his father. I realize there were different rules for men and women in that era. Acceptable behavior for a man was totally abhorred in women. Despite her deafness, Mom would stand toe to toe to defend herself or her sisters, who feared their father and, as a result, caught many a beating for things that they did.

Mom told me most of these stories when I was a young boy. I guess she was trying to distinguish herself from her father, hoping I would see her as a more lenient, tolerant person. Many a conversation would begin with the words; "If I did that my father would …"

Mom contracted diphtheria when she was 16. The high fever destroyed the nerves in her ears, and within a year or so she was totally deaf. She had been chastised, punished and slapped countless times during that year, as her grades deteriorated to the point at which she was barely getting by in school. She had always been an A student, and so grandpa dismissed it as laziness, nothing more. When it became obvious that she had lost most of her hearing, her father transformed into a caring parent, searching out doctors and remedies to make her whole again. Part of this change in him was caused by immense guilt. Ultimately, he was told that there was no treatment for nerve deafness that had been allowed to deteriorate for well over a year. Mom was never again victimized by her father. He became tolerant of her going forward. She, however, would never forget.

When I look back at her life now, I begin to understand what made Mom tick. She would assume the alpha role in her family to ensure that she would never be the victim again. My father was the perfect passive personality to fill the role of husband, do her bidding and rarely challenge her. Her son, her only child, would be molded by her alone, ensuring that I never became what she feared most. Her intentions were good, but, sadly, she could never remove the past that made her what she is today. I've lived my life vowing to be different, and I have to some degree achieved that goal. Good intentions aside, I've made my own mistakes with my children. I've spent 12 years documenting my life in these pages, and the process has proven to be therapeutic. The bitterness has been transformed into acceptance and understanding.

Mom, I finally understand! I am at peace with you and your love for me. Most importantly, I am at peace with myself.

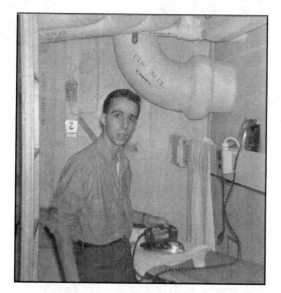

Navy days, 1962